The Politics of Federal Aid to Education in 1965

A Study in Political Innovation

EDUCATION IN LARGE CITIES SERIES

Alan K. Campbell, *Series Editor*

PHILIP MERANTO is assistant professor of government and
research associate in the public administration and metropolitan affairs program at Southern Illinois University,
Edwardsville. He holds a D.S.S. degree from Syracuse
University.

The Politics of Federal Aid
to Education in 1965

A Study in Political Innovation

PHILIP MERANTO

SYRACUSE UNIVERSITY PRESS

Published by
Syracuse University Press
Syracuse, New York

First edition 1967

Library of Congress
Catalog Card: 67-16846

*Manufactured in the
United States of America*

FOR MY PARENTS

Foreword

Improving the quality of public education in America's large central cities is one of the most important domestic problems facing this country. It is within the central cities that many of the disadvantaged groups are concentrated; and partly because of this concentration the largest cities, more than any other type of governmental unit, are facing complex and difficult fiscal and social problems.

The *Education in Large Cities Series* represents an attempt to isolate and analyze policies and policy-making in America's large-city educational systems. The volumes are based on findings of the Large City Education Systems Study, sponsored by the Carnegie Corporation of New York. The statements made and views expressed are solely the responsibility of the authors. This study was conducted by the Metropolitan Studies Program of the Maxwell Graduate School of Citizenship and Public Affairs, Syracuse University, and extended from September 1, 1964 to August 31, 1966.

The central emphasis of the study was on the economics and politics of large-city education. Five large cities, New York, Chicago, Boston, San Francisco, and Atlanta, were selected to receive extensive examination. The economics portion of the study concerned the public financing of education and the interrelation between the inputs and outputs of large-city schools, while the political analysis ranged from the forces involved in acquiring federal funds for education to the role of teachers' organizations in making educational policy.

The authors of the volumes in this series are not experts in educational techniques. They are, rather, students of economics, political science, and administration who have applied the techniques of their disciplines to the analysis of that most expensive of all domestic functions, education.

They have recognized that a combination of educational need and fiscal poverty constitutes an important obstacle to this country's efforts to provide sufficient and equal educational opportunities for all its citizens. Yet, nearly every desirable goal of American society is to some degree dependent on the accomplishment of these educational objectives. For example, economic growth is dependent on allocating sufficient resources to the development and training of the nation's youth. Moreover, the new and complex tasks which must be undertaken by government require a sophisticated electorate. This sophistication must be developed, in the first instance, by education of a quality yet to be achieved in the field of social studies. These are but two examples of the crucial role educational systems must play if this country's potential is to be realized. The performance of this role is much more difficult in the largest cities of the nation than elsewhere—with the possible exception of the rural South.

Although not part of the original design, it was inevitable that policy implications would emerge from each of the individual studies. The degree to which these are emphasized varies from volume to volume, but the summary volume, the last in the series, does attempt to draw all these implications together and to extract from them the policy innovations necessary if city education is to accomplish its assigned tasks.

Any research effort of this magnitude involves literally hundreds of people. These include not only the members of the research staff but many others whose cooperation was crucial to the success of the project. The author's preface to each volume will give appropriate acknowledgment to those who helped with that particular volume, but it is necessary to mention here a few individuals and institutions vital to the entire undertaking.

Without the financial support of the Carnegie Corporation of New York, the Large City Education Systems Study would not have been possible. Equally crucial was the cooperation of the five city school systems in which the large-city study had a representative for nearly two years. In every case, the personnel of the system extended full cooperation and made every possible effort to assist the Study representatives in carrying out their assignments. Without implying their endorsement of the findings of this Study, thanks are extended to each superintendent and his staff: Atlanta, Mr. John W. Letson; Boston, Mr. William W. Ohrenberger; Chicago, Mr. Benjamin Willis; New York City, Mr. Calvin E. Gross and Mr. Bernard E. Donovan; and San Francisco, Mr. Harold Spears.

Holding the whole operation together, and smoothing the administrative path for all members of the staff, was the executive secretary of the Metropolitan Studies Program, Mrs. Jane Rood. Every member of the Study's staff, and particularly its director, is in her debt.

ALAN K. CAMPBELL, *Director*
Metropolitan Studies Program, Syracuse University

Preface

This study was conducted as part of the Carnegie Corporation sponsored research project dealing with Large City Education Systems undertaken by the Metropolitan Studies Program of the Maxwell Graduate School of Citizenship and Public Affairs, Syracuse University. The over-all project was formulated on the premise that the educational difficulties confronting central city school systems constitute one of the nation's most vital domestic problems.

Among the several reports that resulted from this project, at least two are concerned explicitly with delineating various aspects of the fiscal needs of large-city schools while the remaining reports treat topics that carry fiscal implications. The picture that emerges from these reports is disturbing. Central city schools are rapidly becoming engulfed by so-called disadvantaged students who require costly special educational services, yet the cities find themselves without the necessary fiscal resources to meet these needs. It is clearly indicated that city school systems require a considerable amount of additional intergovernmental aid if they are to fulfill their functions. However, state aid flows in greater quantity to the more affluent suburban districts, and until very recently federal school aid was meager and not responsive to the special plight of urban districts.

In 1965 the United States Congress enacted the Elementary and Secondary Education Act, which represents the national government's response to the educational distress of cities. This act constitutes a major breakthrough in the long and controversial fight concerning federal aid to education and promises to be a new major financial commitment of the federal government to the education function, particularly in urban areas. The primary focus of this volume centers on analyzing the politics surrounding the passage of this legislation. The study identifies and examines the various factors that blocked previous attempts to secure legislation and highlights the social and political changes that contributed to the success of federal aid proponents in 1965.

There are a number of individuals to whom I would like to express my gratitude for giving freely of their time and talent to aid me in making this a better study. I wish to thank the several representatives of national organizations in Washington, D.C., for finding time in busy schedules to discuss the issue with me from their individual perspectives. The conception of the study was improved considerably as a result of discussions with members of the Carnegie project during the conference held in the fall of 1965. A special note of thanks is due to Professor Frank Munger, a member of the staff, who provided counsel on several occasions. Professor David Ranney graciously took time out from his own investigation to read and discuss this report with me and offered many useful suggestions. I also benefited from many related discussions with Professor Seymour Sacks, who has contributed greatly to my understanding of the points of contact between economics and politics. I would like to express particular appreciation to Professor Alan K. Campbell, who originally suggested the topic and who supplied invaluable guidance and encouragement. Finally, I am grateful to my wife Barbara, who typed the drafts of the manuscript and who provided the support that only a wife can give.

In addition, grateful acknowledgment is made to the following for their kind permission to quote from works held in copyright:

Christian Century—Quotation reprinted with permission from editorial of February 1, 1961, issue of *Christian Century*.

Earl Latham and the American Political Science Association—Quotation reprinted by permission of both author and publisher from "The Group Basis of Politics," *American Political Science Review* (June, 1963).

McGraw-Hill Book Company—Quotation reprinted with permission from *Obstacle Course on Capitol Hill* by Robert Bendiner (New York: McGraw-Hill, 1964).

Teachers College, Columbia University—Quotation reprinted with the permission of the publisher from "The Disadvantaged Child and the Learning Process," by Martin Deutsch in A. Harry Passow, editor, *Education in Depressed Areas* (New York: Teachers College Press, 1963), © 1963 by Teachers College, Columbia University.

Naturally, I assume responsibility for all shortcomings of the book.

The research reported herein was financed in part by a grant from the U.S. Office of Education.

PHILIP MERANTO

Edwardsville, Illinois
January, 1967

Contents

Tables

Figures

I. Political Innovation: A Conceptual Framework

INTRODUCTION

> I am very proud of your House of Representatives and your United States Senate, and I know everyone is applauding the historic action that the Congress has just taken. Since 1870, almost a hundred years ago, we have been trying to do what we have just done—pass an elementary school bill for all the children of America.[1]

Thus President Lyndon B. Johnson, on April 9, 1965, reacted to the announcement that the United States Congress had approved the Elementary and Secondary Education Act of 1965. A few days later, while seated outside the former one-room schoolhouse at Stonewall, Texas, where he first attended classes, the President signed the bill into law. He emphasized his satisfaction with the new legislation and its supporters by commenting:

> As President, I believe deeply that no law I have signed or will ever sign means more to the future of our nation. . . . I predict that all of those of both parties of Congress who supported the enactment of this legislation will be remembered in history as men and women who began a new day of greatness in American society.[2]

The President's stress on the innovative nature of this legislation is quite understandable to those who are familiar with the history of past efforts to enact a program of general federal aid for elementary and secondary education.[3] For nearly a century the national legislature considered dozens of proposals designed to originate such a program; yet none were approved. The various proposals invariably were accompanied by a host of controversial issues that made majority consensus on federal aid to education extremely elusive. Many of the proposi-

[1] *The New York Times,* April 10, 1965, p. 1.
[2] *Ibid.,* April 12, 1965, pp. 1, 22.
[3] Although this exact wording will not always be used, owing to style and space considerations, this study is primarily concerned with the kind of federal aid which is referred to as "general aid for elementary and secondary education."

1

tions became involved with some combination of explosive questions such as federal control of education, the granting of federal funds to segregated schools, the distribution of federal aid to private educational institutions, and the allocation of federal funds among the states. Indeed, this area of national public policy has been so plagued by a variety of sensitive topics that careful students of the issue consistently predicted that the passage of a federal aid for education bill was quite unlikely. For example, at the conclusion of a detailed and insightful analysis of the 1961 congressional deliberation concerning federal aid to elementary and secondary education, political scientist Hugh Douglas Price wrote:

> The bitterness of the 1961 legislative struggle and the difficulties of reaching a consensus on the status of nonpublic schools will not soon be forgotten. In private, many school-aid supporters admitted that federal aid of the sort proposed by President Kennedy was dead, not just for the 87th Congress, but probably for the decade of the 1960's.[4]

The pessimism expressed by Price is not an isolated conclusion. A more historical study of the federal aid to education issue, written by Frank Munger and Richard Fenno, clearly illustrates that the 1961 setback was only the most recent of a long string of proponent failures. Their account of the numerous attempts to enact a federal aid to education program and of the concomitant controversies and pitfalls surrounding this issue suggests how improbable passage of such legislation was thought to be. Munger and Fenno characterized the movement for federal aid as one that seemed to continue but not progress and concluded that:

> For close to a century the federal aid story-line has run on without a break, rather in the manner of a daytime television serial. There is no particular reason to assume the end is now in sight, and some good reasons to suspect that federal aid will not be approved within the immediate future.[5]

Other commentators also have noted the seemingly endless attempts, yet proponent failures, that have been typical of the school-aid movement. For instance, Robert Bendiner, who was interested in presenting an argument for congressional institutional reform, decided that for purposes of illustration he required "an issue with a long, varied, and frustrating life history, and had no trouble therefore in choosing federal

---

[4] "Race, Religion and the Rules Committee: The Kennedy Aid-to-Education Bills," in Alan F. Westin (ed.), *The Uses of Power* (New York: Harcourt, Brace and World, Inc., 1961), p. 67.

[5] Frank J. Munger and Richard F. Fenno, Jr., *National Politics and Federal Aid to Education* (Syracuse: Syracuse University Press, 1961), p. 170.

aid to the elementary and secondary schools of the country."[6] This issue served his purposes well, for Bendiner had little difficulty in demonstrating how the congressional machinery may be utilized to block legislation that lacks what he calls "a determined and overwhelming majority." After reviewing the recent history of the school-aid campaign, he also made the point that the probability of passing a primary and secondary aid for education bill in the near future was minimal. In his judgment, only a "miraculous" set of circumstances could produce such an occurrence. The likelihood of this ideal pattern emerging is expressed in the following manner:

> From all that has gone before, it can be said that the spontaneous arrangement of circumstances is possible—but only in the same way that it is possible for pigments thrown at a canvas to shape themselves into the "Last Supper." That is, it may happen, but it is not a good bet, and to have to count on it for the success of legislation approaches the preposterous.[7]

Despite almost one hundred years of proponent failure, and despite the informed opinions expressed above, Congress, during the spring of 1965, approved a bill that has been referred to as the first program of general aid for elementary and secondary education in America's history. In view of the history of the school-aid movement, particularly the most recent failures to enact such legislation, the perplexing questions which emerge concern how and why the congressional action of 1965 resulted in success. More specifically, what accounts for the fact that a school-aid bill (1) successfully reached the House floor for a vote in 1965 and (2) gained a majority vote to reverse the most recent proponent defeat of 1961 (see Table 1)?[8] This study attempts to answer these questions.

THE MEANING OF GENERAL AID

First, it is necessary to point out that the legislation under examination is a major departure in national education policy. Some students of federal aid for education may reasonably argue that the Elementary and Secondary Education Act of 1965 is not an authentic general aid to education program, which differs significantly from the pattern of

[6] *Obstacle Course on Capitol Hill* (New York: McGraw-Hill Book Co., 1964), p. 7.

[7] *Ibid.*, p. 192.

[8] The emphasis on action in the House of Representatives stems from the fact that proponents of school aid have been relatively successful in passing bills in the Senate during the post-World War II period but have encountered stiff resistance in the House for reasons which will become apparent throughout this study.

TABLE 1
HOUSE VOTE ON FEDERAL AID TO EDUCATION, 1961 AND 1965

	1961			1965			
	Yea	Nay	% Yea	Yea	Nay	% Yea	Gain in Yea Votes
Northern Democrats	143	12	92	197	4	98	+54
Southern Democrats	21	70	23	31	53	37	+10
Total Democrats	164	82	67	228	57	80	+64
Republicans	6	160	4	35	96	27	+29
Total Vote	170	242	41	263	153	63	+93

SOURCE: Compiled from *Congressional Quarterly Almanac,* 1961 and 1965.

limited and specialized program aid. They may affirm that it is comparable to the Smith-Hughes Act of 1917, which set up the initial program of federal grants-in-aid to promote vocational education in precollegiate schools, or to the Lanham Act of 1940, and subsequent "impacted area" legislation, which provided federal funds for school districts experiencing enrollment increases due to the presence of federal personnel and their families. This is a fair position to take since the Education Act of 1965 does have a somewhat specialized and "impacted area" characteristic.

Title I of the law, which accounts for about $1.1 billion of the approximately $1.3 billion authorized for the fiscal year 1966, provides for grants to local school districts having concentrations of children from low-income families. Title I aid is calculated by multiplying 50 per cent of the state's average per pupil expenditures for the school year 1963–64 by the total number of five- to seventeen-year-old children in the local school district who are from families with annual incomes below $2,000 and from families with higher incomes resulting from aid-to-dependent-children relief payments. Local school districts do not automatically receive the aid but must submit, to their state education department for approval, plans "to expand and improve their educational programs by various means (including preschool programs) which contribute particularly to meeting the special educational needs of educationally deprived children."[9] Consequently, this is aid to school districts that are impacted by poverty-stricken families and is, in that sense, a specialized aid program.[10]

[9] U.S., Congress, Senate, Committee on Labor and Public Welfare, *Elementary and Secondary Education Act of 1965,* 89th Cong., 1st Sess., 1965, p. 25.
[10] See the Appendix for a summary of the complete law.

Part of the difficulty in determining whether such a program is general aid or not revolves around the imprecise usage of the term "general." Evidently, the most general type of federal aid would be aid granted to school districts in a manner similar to the distribution of most state aid for education. That is, all school districts would receive some aid, the amount dependent upon the state's particular formula, with the funds being expended among various categories at the discretion of the local school district. This kind of aid is referred to as general because all districts receive some proportion of the total and because the local districts have the right to decide how it is to be spent.

Confusion arises because the school construction and teacher salary bills, which have been presented to the national legislature for the past decade or so, have been referred to as general aid even though it is clear that the local school districts would be compelled to use the funds in specialized expenditure categories. In this context, the Education Act of 1965 is certainly as general as the construction and salary proposals, probably more so since both types of expenditures are possible under Title I, as are many other expenditures for activities related to improving the education of culturally deprived children.[11]

A number of other factors also indicate the general nature of the 1965 legislation. Funds under Title I, for example, will be allocated to both public and private school districts in at least 95 per cent of the nation's counties; grants under the other titles of the act will presumably benefit all school districts.[12] Title II grants provided for a five-year program to enable school libraries to purchase textbooks and other instructional materials for use by children and teachers in all public and private elementary and secondary schools. The provisions of Title III establish a five-year program of grants to states for the creation of supplementary educational centers and services which are to be available to both public and private school students. Titles IV and V give aid indirectly to elementary and secondary education by supplying federal funds for educational research and for the strengthening of state education departments.

In addition, the $1.3 billion authorized for the fiscal year 1966 represents a figure that is considerably higher than the estimated $497 million expended by the federal government on all its various elementary and secondary aid programs in 1965 (see Table 2). The Education Act of 1965, therefore, almost triples the federal fiscal commitment to primary and secondary education. In this sense, it appears that "the foot

---

[11] For a listing of the various programs possible under Title I provisions, see: Senate Committee on Labor and Public Welfare, *op. cit.*, pp. 636–37.

[12] *Ibid.*, p. 894.

in the door," which fiscal conservatives have resisted for so long, has been inserted.

It is clear from the quotations included earlier in this chapter that President Johnson perceived the law as a major new school-aid bill, as did many congressmen, including Senator Jacob Javits (Republican, New York), who termed the bill "the most comprehensive and far-reaching education program ever sent to Congress."[13] *Congressional*

TABLE 2

FEDERAL FINANCIAL ASSISTANCE TO EDUCATION, 1956–66 (IN MILLIONS)

Year	Elementary and Secondary Education	Higher Education	Total
1956	$ 123.9	$ 5.1	$ 129.0
1958	225.7	5.1	230.8
1960	327.6	70.5	398.1
1962	383.2	132.3	515.5
1964	409.1	180.3	589.4
1965	497.6	706.0	1203.4
1966	520.1[a]	949.1[a]	1469.2[a]
1966	1281.0[b]		

[a] Estimate.

[b] Elementary and Secondary Education Act of 1965.

SOURCE: Senate Committee on Labor and Public Welfare, *Elementary and Secondary Education Act of 1965,* 89th Cong., 1st Sess., 1965, p. 98.

Quarterly arrived at a similar conclusion in its 1965 special report on the role of the federal government in education, stating: "The first general aid to education bill ever to clear Congress was enacted this year."[14]

Regardless of whether the legislation should or should not be termed general, the crucial fact remains that a significant and substantial set of political changes occurred between 1961 and 1965 which considerably altered the relationship between the federal government and education. Given the present and projected role of the education function in American society, it is not unreasonable to suggest that this new commitment of federal aid to education may, in the long run, represent the most important change in national domestic policy since the New Deal period. The importance of this commitment justifies a study of the factors contributing to it.

A SYSTEMS APPROACH TO POLITICAL INNOVATION

In attempting to explain the advent of such a potentially far-reaching alteration in national policy and legislative action, it is necessary to

[13] Quoted in *The New York Times,* January 13, 1965, p. 21.

[14] Congressional Quarterly Service, *Federal Role in Education* (Washington, D.C.: 1965), p. 31.

consider the more fundamental question of how major innovation occurs in the American political system. Unfortunately for the student of political change, the trend in political science toward systematic empirical and theoretical inquiry has not included an emphasis in explaining major change. In addition, and more relevant to this study, the various scholarly approaches to national legislative politics, such as the case study approach to a bill[15] or the studies that focus on functional and systems analysis of sublegislation units,[16] also fail to stress what influences the national legislature to reverse its position on a long-standing issue. The former approach tends to emphasize a detailed empirical examination of the "full life" of a particular bill to illuminate the congressional processing of legislation, while the latter generally utilizes an equilibrium model dealing with conflict adjustment and consensus building at the subsystem level rather than a model that stresses major innovation at the more-encompassing legislative level. Lacking an explicit model of major political change at this more general unit of analysis, the legislative level, the researcher may either invent a unique model or construct a conceptual framework through the adaptation of existing concepts. The latter strategy has been selected in this study. More specifically, an attempt will be made to combine elements of the systems approach to political behavior at the societal level, as developed by such theorists as David Easton and William Mitchell,[17] with aspects of a legislative model constructed by John C. Wahlke and his colleagues.[18]

[15] See, for example, Stephen K. Bailey, *Congress Makes a Law* (New York: Columbia University Press, 1950), and Daniel M. Berman, *A Bill Becomes a Law* (New York: The Macmillan Company, 1966).

[16] Examples of this more recent approach to national legislative politics may be found in some of the studies included in Robert Peabody and Nelson Polsby (eds.), *New Perspectives on the House of Representatives* (Chicago: Rand McNally & Company, 1963). See also Ralph Huitt, "The Congressional Committee: A Case Study," *American Political Science Review,* XLVIII (June, 1954), 340–65; Charles O. Jones, "The Role of the Congressional Subcommittee," *Midwest Journal of Political Science,* VI (November, 1962), 327–444; George Goodwin, "Subcommittees, The Miniature Legislatures of Congress," *American Political Science Review,* LVI (September, 1962), 596–604; and John F. Manley, "The House Committee on Ways and Means: Conflict Management in a Congressional Committee," *American Political Science Review,* LIX (December, 1965), 927–39.

[17] See David Easton, "An Approach to the Analysis of Political Systems," *World Politics,* IX (April, 1957), 383–400; *A Framework for Political Analysis* (Englewood Cliffs: Prentice-Hall, 1965); *A Systems Analysis of Political Life* (New York: John Wiley & Sons, Inc., 1965); and William C. Mitchell, *The American Polity* (New York: The Free Press of Glencoe, 1962).

[18] John C. Wahlke, Heinz Enlau, William Buchanan, and Leroy C. Ferguson, *The Legislative System* (New York: John Wiley & Sons, Inc., 1962). For a related discussion see Edward A. Shils, "The Legislator and His Environment," *The University of Chicago Law Review,* XVIII (Spring, 1951), 571–84.

Basic Propositions

Probably the most basic point is that the systems approach posits the proposition that the subject matter of political science may be viewed as a system because it is designed to focus on the set of interrelationships among political actors and institutions. These actors, working through the institutions, produce authoritative decisions concerning which competing political goals and aspirations will be written into public policy and consequently will be enforced by the legitimate power of the state. Such behavior and structures may be viewed as a system because the various parts are interrelated in such a manner that variation in any one part has an impact on the remaining sectors.

A second basic point is that the systems approach is essentially descriptive in character. It attempts to indicate the relationship among various parts of the political system; thus, at this stage, it is more useful as an organizational scheme than a predictive model.

Another fundamental proposition of the systems model is that a unit such as the political system may be sufficiently and profitably differentiated from the other social systems operating in a society. To identify the political system as an analytical category, it is necessary to abstract those aspects of human interaction that are essentially political. "What distinguishes political interactions from all other kinds of social interactions is that they are predominantly oriented toward the authoritative allocation of values for a society."[19] Clearly, the political system overlaps with the other social systems in a society insofar as the individuals involved are members of various subsystems. Consequently, the legislator may be considered a member of the economic system, the religious system, and so forth; however, an attempt is made to isolate and analyze that portion of his behavior which is most directly related to the authoritative allocation of values in order to assess its impact within the political system. Theoretically, when such a process is completed successfully for all members of a society it is possible to delineate the interactions that compose the political system of the society, realizing, of course, that the boundary between the political system and other subsystems is somewhat hazy and that all societal systems are highly interrelated.

Although a political system is distinguishable from the environment in which it exists, it is an open system. In other words, it is open to influences from other subsystems within the society and extrasocietal sub-

[19] Easton, *A Framework for Political Analysis*, p. 50. For a discussion of additional systems operating in society, see Talcott Parsons, *The Social System* (New York: The Free Press, 1951) and Talcott Parsons and Edward Shils (eds.), *Toward a General Theory of Action* (New York: Harper and Row, 1951).

systems. Thus, phenomena, both physical and social, that occur outside the boundaries of a political system may play an important, and in some cases a crucial, role in influencing the manner of interaction within the system and the consequent outputs. Therefore, an inflation in the economy, a shift in cultural values, a redistribution of population, or an international crisis each may have important implications for a political system.

Under particular circumstances environmental events and conditions are transmitted to a political system in the form of political demands and as potential sources of stress which generally stimulate the internal structures and processes within the system to regulate or cope with the stress produced by the demands. Put more formally, the environmental conditions shape the inputs to a political system in which they are converted by the internal mechanism, e.g., the legislature, into outputs. It is important to note that occurrences within a political system are also capable of producing sufficient stress to require a response in the form of outputs.[20] For example, a rapid shift in the relative powers between the legislative and executive branches of a political system may produce a state of tension that can influence the nature of outputs.

Within the systems approach, the term "outputs" refers only to the authoritative allocation of values such as legislative laws, executive orders, judicial rulings, administrative decisions, and all other decrees that are backed by the legitimate power of the state.

The discharge of authoritative outputs is not terminal; once the outputs have emerged from the system, they have a feedback effect on the general environment and potentially the political system itself. This feedback process becomes crucial to the persistence of a political system since it provides a flow of information to the authorities within a system, allowing them to assess and respond to the impact previous outputs have had on the original demands made upon the system. An emphasis on the concept of process is inherent in this framework. It is demonstrated by the linkage of outputs to new inputs and the political system through subsequent feedback; by the relationship between the political system and its environment; and by the genesis of stress within the system.

Methodology

The task remaining is to adjust this framework, which pertains to a political system at the total societal level, to the national legislative level. Such a shift involves reducing the unit of analysis from the total societal politi-

---

[20] In order to distinguish these internal, political stresses from the external, environmental stresses, Easton has suggested the term "withinputs" for the former. *Ibid.*, pp. 114–15.

cal system to a subpolitical system. For purposes of this study, the subpolitical system that will be the focus of analysis is the congressional component of the national government. As has already been implied in the preceding discussion, changes in outputs emerging from a political system may result from changes in the environment and/or changes within the system itself. The basic argument developed in this study is that the new output—the Elementary and Secondary Education Act of 1965—was the result of a mixture of past and immediate changes, both in the environment and within the political system, which came together in a unique grouping capable of generating a new major public policy that had long been blocked by a variety of factors. The variables in both categories, the environment and the political system itself, which appear to hold the most promise for explaining the nature of the changes and how they contributed to the output under consideration, are identified and analyzed.

Within the environmental category, two subcategories are considered; one may be termed "circumstantial conditions,"[21] the other "demand articulators." The first refers to the fact that a legislative system exists at any specific time within a generalized environment which it shares with the other social systems of society. The conditions that characterize the general environment, however, may have special implications for the functioning of the political system. For example, the political system functions differently if the legislature is operating during a period of economic growth or distress, or during a period of rapid social change.

Throughout the struggle for federal aid to education, proponents have attempted to put the rationale for federal aid into a context that reflected a condition in the general society with "crisislike" implications for the education function. The proportion of selective service rejections during the World War periods produced demands for federal aid to education in 1918 and 1943; the social and economic conditions of the Depression stimulated emergency aid to education in the 1930's; and the postwar teacher shortage and baby boom of the 1940's and 1950's created the context for the most recent general aid bills.

This study illustrates that at least three environmental conditions which became prevalent between 1961 and 1965 altered the rationale underpinning federal aid to education. These three circumstantial conditions include the "rediscovery" of poverty in American society, the trend of metropolitanization and its consequences for the education function, and the civil rights movement. The nature of these factors, their

---

[21] This particular concept and the consequent framework follows in a general manner the approach suggested by Wahlke *et al.*, *The Legislative System*, especially pp. 3–29.

implications for education, and their relationships to the Education Act of 1965 are explored.

The circumstantial conditions in the environment surrounding the legislative system may be instrumental in creating input demands on the system in two ways: They may have a direct impact on legislators who perceive the actual conditions as political demands requiring responses; or the conditions may be filtered through "demand articulators," the second subcategory in the general environment.[22]

FIGURE 1

A MODEL OF LEGISLATIVE CHANGE

Environmental Changes		Changes Within the Legislative System	
A. Circumstantial Conditions			
1. The Rediscovery of Poverty	New → Inputs	A. Alteration of Party Ratios on House Education Committee	
2. The Metropolitan Trend			
3. The Civil Rights Movement		B. Change from Barden to Powell as Chairman	New → Output
B. Major Demand Articulators		C. Enlargement of House Rules Committee	
1. Constituents	New → Inputs		
2. Organized Interest Groups			
3. Political Parties			
4. The President			

There are at least four groups which may be identified as demand articulators that perform the function of providing legislators with sources of legislative input. Comprising this environmental subcategory are constituents, organized interest groups, the principal political parties, and the chief executive. All four have an influential impact on the nature of interaction within the legislative system and the kinds of outputs that emerge from it.

The various changes that occurred among these factors, and their subsequent influences on the outcome of the 1965 bill, are discussed. Constituents' opinions on federal school aid, as reflected through public opinion polls, are examined over time; the interest groups for and against

---

[22] It is possible, of course, for the legislative system to receive the same demands simultaneously from circumstantial conditions and the major demand articulators.

education aid in 1961 and 1965 are contrasted; the past and more recent postures of the major political parties concerning the issue are examined; finally, the views of postwar Presidents on aid to education and their relative commitments to the cause are compared.

As the previous discussion has indicated, changes in the environment surrounding the legislature represent one principal source of explanation concerning a new policy output; the other main origin of innovation may be found in changes that occurred within the system itself. It would be impossible to take into account all the changes within the political system that have occurred over such a period of years. Therefore, to make the analysis in this study manageable, three major alterations, which according to past studies have been instrumental in influencing the outcome of federal aid to education bills, are identified and examined. They are: (1) the alteration in the proportion of Democrats and Republicans on the House Committee on Education and Labor in 1959, (2) the change from Graham Barden to Adam Clayton Powell as chairman of that committee in 1961, and (3) the increase in membership of the House Rules Committee in 1961.

In summary, this investigation has been put into the context of political innovation because it involves an attempt to identify and analyze the most significant factors contributing to the enactment of a bill that represents a new major policy commitment of the federal government. First, an examination is made of the environmental changes that appear to have influenced the decision; second, a discussion of the relevant system changes is presented; and third, the factors are related to one another.

II. Poverty, City Schools, and Civil Rights: The New Rationale for Federal Aid

BACKGROUND

One of the characteristics of a legislative system is its openness; that is, its responsiveness to conditions existing in its environment which have been converted to political demands either by members within the system or by demand articulators. Generally, this means that individuals or groups have identified particular social, economic, or political conditions which they perceive as problematic and have utilized whatever political resources they possess to have these conditions altered by governmental action. A central focus of political science has been on those who are successful in realizing their demands and the reasons for their success, or "who gets what, when, and how." Although the answers may be fragmentary, one factor appears to be clear: The proponents of a goal increase their chances of victory if they are able to convincingly relate their objectives to the alleviation of some general societal "crisis."

A recent illustration of this principle is the enactment of the National Defense Education Act (NDEA) of 1958. After the Soviet Union launched its first earth satellite, Sputnik, on October 4, 1957, grave warnings were made in many corners that the United States had lagged seriously behind the Soviets in the field of science, thus presenting a national security crisis. To deal with this situation proponents of a federal education program were successful in linking this "crisis" to their aim; by September, 1958, President Dwight D. Eisenhower had signed the NDEA into law with the comment that it would "do much to strengthen our American system of education so that it can meet the broad and increasing demands imposed upon it by considerations of basic national security."[1]

The supporters of federal aid to elementary and secondary education

[1] Quoted in Congressional Quarterly Service, *Federal Role in Education*, p. 10.

have not ignored the "crisis" strategy. Throughout the twentieth century they have attempted to utilize a variety of pressing social conditions to strengthen the urgency of their political demands. For example, they pointed to the high rate of selective service rejections due to illiteracy during both World War periods in an attempt to dramatize the frequency of illiteracy in American society and the inadequacy of the response made to this condition by the education system. In more recent years proponents of federal aid have used these arguments plus the educational problems resulting from the post-World War II teacher and classroom shortage to bolster their request for federal support of education.[2]

During the last decade or so those arguing for federal aid have tended to stress above all else the teacher and classroom shortage and a series of interrelated conditions which they feel warrant increased federal support for education. Generally, the argument has been presented in the following terms:

(1) The education function is in a state of crisis resulting from the baby boom of the early 1940's and the postwar period in general. The impact of the baby boom on schools is reflected in public school enrollment statistics which show that enrollment actually declined between 1930 and 1950 from 25.6 million to 25.1 million. However, by the school year 1959–60 enrollment jumped to 36.1 million, an increase of about 43 per cent in one decade.[3]

(2) The enrollment explosion has caused a serious shortage of classrooms; has increased the size of classes; and has contributed, along with low salaries, to the failure to attract and keep a sufficient number of qualified individuals in the profession of education.[4] Consequently, many

[2] The efforts for federal action during the two war periods are discussed in some detail in Anne Gibson Buis, *An Historical Study of the Role of the Federal Government in the Financial Support of Education, with Special Reference to Legislative Proposals and Action* (unpublished doctoral dissertation, Ohio State University, 1953), and William Alexander Mitchell, *Federal Aid for Primary and Secondary Education* (unpublished doctoral dissertation, Princeton University, 1948).

[3] Individuals testifying before congressional committees have used a variety of statistics at different times to illustrate this trend. These figures are taken from: U.S., Department of Health, Education, and Welfare, Office of Education, *Digest of Educational Statistics* (Washington: U.S. Government Printing Office, 1965), p. 10.

[4] Much debate has centered around the statistics that supposedly support these patterns. The National Education Association, for example, claimed in 1961 that there was a 140,000 classroom backlog. The U.S. Chamber of Commerce, on the other hand, argued that classroom construction was outstripping increased enrollment and that, if there were a shortage, it was much smaller. For both points of view see: U.S., House, Committee on Education and Labor, *Federal Aid to Schools,* 87th Cong., 1st Sess., 1961, pp. 165–70, 282–85.

schools are characterized by overcrowded conditions, the operation of double shifts, and undermanned instructional staffs.

(3) The federal government has a responsibility to help relieve these problems because of their implications for national welfare. National wealth and economic productivity have been related to the increased educational level of the population. A sound education system also underpins the nation's scientific and defense capabilities. In addition, the society has become increasingly interdependent, particularly through the increased internal mobility of the work force and school population; consequently, the quality of education in any one part of the country has implications for the rest of the society and is of national concern.

(4) Not only does the federal government have a responsibility to support education, it also has the necessary resources. Local school districts and state governments have had their fiscal resources strained to the limit by demands for improved educational and noneducational services. The federal government with its superior tax base is in a position to provide relief for state and local governments while simultaneously increasing the nation's potential through a strengthened education system.[5]

Enrollment explosion, classroom shortage, teacher shortage, fiscal strain, and national well-being—these conditions constitute the environmental factors which recent proponents of federal aid have used to support their political demands. Judged by the results, the reasoning of school-aid supporters has not been convincing to the majority of the decision-makers within the national legislature. Apparently, the educational crisis they have depicted has not been sufficiently urgent to secure positive legislation.

How is the enactment of the Education Act of 1965 related to these arguments for federal aid? Did the environmental conditions referred to worsen and thus provide the proponents with a stronger foundation from which to present their position? Did the conditions remain relatively the same with the supporters of aid pleading their case with more force and intensity? Or were new environmental conditions introduced into the picture which allowed federal aid supporters to construct a novel context for their demands? The latter interpretation seems the most plausible.

Instead of arguing for federal aid on the grounds reviewed above, proponents of federal aid to education in 1965 utilized a new rationale which centered around such terms as "the poverty-stricken family," "the poverty cycle," "the disadvantaged student," and "the crisis confronting

---

[5] For a typical presentation of this argument see the testimony of Carl J. Megel, president of the American Federation of Teachers, before the House Committee on Education and Labor during 1961. *Ibid.*, p. 267.

urban school systems." To appreciate why this shift in emphasis occurred it is necessary to review the emergence of a set of social and economic patterns which have become salient public issues in the mid-1960's. Specifically, it is necessary to discuss three subjects that characterize this time period: the "rediscovery" of poverty in the United States, the recognition of America as a metropolitan society, and the civil rights movement.

THE "REDISCOVERY" OF POVERTY

Awareness and concern with the problem of poverty in America, the land of abundance, are not recent phenomena. In his volume, *Progress and Poverty,* Henry George described the United States of the post-Civil War period as a land where "amid the greatest accumulation of wealth, men die of starvation and puny infants suckle dry breasts."[6] In 1890, reporter Jacob Riis presented, in his widely quoted book *How the Other Half Lives,* a vivid portrayal of the degrading living conditions of New York City slum dwellers;[7] and President Franklin D. Roosevelt in his State of the Union Message of 1933 made his now-famous reference to the "one third of the nation that is ill-clothed, ill-housed, and ill-nourished."

The recognition of impoverishment in the United States was considerably obscured by the economic prosperity of World War II and the postwar years. Indeed, by 1958, John Kenneth Galbraith, author of *The Affluent Society,* one of the best-selling books of that year, suggested that the widespread poverty which had characterized man's historical experience had been replaced by general well-being in sections of Europe and especially in the United States. He wrote:

> No one would wish to argue that the ideas which interpreted [that] world of grim scarcity would serve equally well for contemporary United States. Poverty was the all-pervasive fact of that world. Obviously it is not of ours.[8]

Although Galbraith recognized that poverty was by no means absent in American society, his book emphasized the implications of affluence. However, those who "rediscovered" poverty in affluent America stressed its pervasive yet concealed and invisible nature. Michael Harrington, who in general provided the impetus for this perspective through his book *The Other America: Poverty in the United States,* argued that America's poor are largely "invisible" to the average American because

6 (New York: Robert Schalenback Foundation, 1940), p. 12.

7 (New York: Hill and Wang, 1957).

8 (New York: New American Library, 1958), p. 14.

the poor are off the main thoroughfares which the ordinary traveler follows; they are isolated physically from affluent suburbia; their relatively adequate clothing hides their poverty; many are the wrong age (too young or too old) to be noticed; and they are invisible politically because they have no organized groups pressing for legislation.[9]

Visual concealment and numerical ambiguity of the poor make the magnitude of poverty in contemporary America difficult to assess. Statistics on poverty may be misleading for a number of reasons such as the income figure used in the definition, the size of families included, the different stages of the life cycle, and the geographic region involved. Given the definitional difficulties, it is not surprising to discover that there is disagreement in the literature over the proportion of the American population that may be considered in the poverty category. In general, the figures most often cited range from a low estimate of about 32 million to a high of about 50 million poverty-stricken individuals. Despite the disagreement over statistics, most of the recent studies on poverty agree that it is a rather widespread and serious phenomenon in America.[10]

The notion that poverty is still an important characteristic of American society discloses only a portion of the situation. The often-repeated theme in the literature is that present-day poverty is a new kind of poverty with new implications.[11] The argument is made that the old poverty group generally was composed of immigrants who had come to a new land with high aspirations and who saw poverty as a temporary state, if not for themselves, at least for their children. Essentially, their anticipation was correct; their arrival coincided with an expanding economy that contained an abundance of unskilled and semiskilled jobs, which made possible economic and social mobility.

In contrast, the new poor are generally internal aliens in a prosperous

[9] (Baltimore: Penguin Books, Inc., 1962), pp. 11–14. For an extension of this theme see Dwight MacDonald, "Our Invisible Poor," *New Yorker,* January 19, 1963.

[10] One of the more rigorous attempts to define poverty and its extent can be found in the monograph by Millie Orshansky, "Counting the Poor; Another Look at the Poverty Profile," *Social Security Bulletin,* January, 1965. See also Ben H. Bagdikian, *In the Midst of Plenty: A New Report on the Poor in America* (New York: Signet Books, 1964); Leon H. Keyserling, *Progress or Poverty: The United States at the Crossroads* (Washington, D.C.: Conference on Economic Progress, 1964); and James N. Morgan *et al., Income and Welfare in the United States* (New York: McGraw-Hill Book Company, Inc., 1962).

[11] For a good summary of this argument see Michael Harrington's introduction to *Poverty in America: A Book of Readings,* ed. Louis A. Ferman, Joyce L. Kornbluh, and Alan Haber (Ann Arbor: The University of Michigan Press, 1965).

society. They include farm workers who have been displaced by mechanization, white and Negro migrants who have moved from backward rural areas to urban slum centers, unskilled and undereducated workers in declining industries, displaced workers who are victims of technological change, and the aged or physically disabled who cannot participate in the labor force. For these individuals, poverty is less likely to be viewed as temporary; they are more inclined to perceive it as a way of life that contains little promise for change. This perception of poverty is related to alterations in the opportunity structure. Unlike that of earlier periods, the labor market of today is unable to absorb great numbers of underskilled and undereducated workers. Thus, objectively, the poor of today have less chance for upward mobility than had the poor of the past. Recognition of this fact by the poor seems to breeds pessimism among them and ultimately among their children. The alarming concern is that this condition of poverty will be passed from one generation to the next.

The educational implication of poverty stems from the correlation between low family income and low educational attainment. Children of the poor are less likely to do well while they attend school and have a greater tendency to leave school before completing a high school education.[12] Their lower educational accomplishments put them at a disadvantage in the labor market which is increasingly demanding more highly educated and skilled workers. Since their educational background fails to prepare them for the requirements of the labor market, it is not surprising that the young poor experience high unemployment rates and receive low wages when they are employed.[13] Their low income, in turn, is associated with a whole range of conditions: residence in substandard and unsanitary housing, inadequate diets, lack of regular medical care, greater incidences of sickness, and absence from work or school which is conducive to perpetuating the whole cycle.

From the perspective of this study, the most important linkage is between the so-called "poverty syndrome" and education as a means for breaking the cycle. As the spotlight was turned again on the extent of poverty in the United States, much attention centered on the "disadvantaged student," "the culturally deprived student," "the underprivileged student," and "the socially impoverished student." A great deal of the writing and discussion focused on what the schools were doing and

[12] For a discussion of this relationship see Patricia Sexton, *Education and Income: Inequalities in Our Public Schools* (New York: The Viking Press, 1962); H. Thomas James, J. Alan Thomas, and Harold J. Dyck, *Wealth, Expenditures, and Decision-Making for Education* (Stanford: Stanford University Press, 1963); and Jesse Burkhead, *Input and Output in Large-City High Schools* (Syracuse: Syracuse University Press, 1967).

[13] Louis A. Ferman *et al., Poverty in America,* pp. 134–85.

neglecting to do to meet the needs of these students.[14] The general line of reasoning that characterizes this literature is captured succinctly by Martin Deutsch:

> Among children who come from lower-class socially impoverished circumstances, there is a high proportion of school failure, school drop-outs, reading and learning disabilities, as well as life adjustment problems. This means not only that these children grow up poorly equipped academically, but also that the effectiveness of the school as a major institution for socialization is diminished.
>
> The thesis here is that the lower-class child enters the school situation so poorly prepared to produce what the school demands that initial failures are almost inevitable, and the school experience becomes negatively rather than positively reinforced. Thus, the child's experience in school does nothing to counteract the invidious influences to which he is exposed in his slum, and sometimes segregated neighborhood.[15]

Educational and other institutions responded to this problem in various ways. In some instances local school districts reallocated portions of their resources to provide special education services for these students, and occasionally the districts were assisted in the development of programs by private foundations.[16] Most recently, and for this study most importantly, school districts have received aid from the federal government under its various antipoverty programs enacted by the Kennedy and Johnson administrations. These programs include the Area Redevelopment Act of 1962, the Vocational Education Act of 1963, and especially the Economic Opportunity Act of 1964. The latter legislation represents the first major program originated by President Johnson in his declared war on poverty. The environmental conditions related to the antipoverty legislation, the rationale underlying it, and its political appeal are not unrelated to the kind of school-aid bill presented to the national legislature in 1965.

This re-emphasis on alleviation of poverty in America and the reliance

[14] For a sampling of this literature see Frank Riessman, *The Culturally Deprived Child* (New York: Harper and Row, 1962); Judith R. Kramer and Seymour Leventman, *Children of the Gilded Ghetto* (New Haven: Yale University Press, 1961); A. Harry Passow (ed.), *Education in Depressed Areas* (New York: Teachers College, Columbia University, 1963); and C. W. Hunnicutt (ed.), *Urban Education and Cultural Deprivation* (Syracuse: Syracuse University Press, 1964).

[15] Martin Deutsch, "The Disadvantaged Child and the Learning Process," in Passow, *Education in Depressed Areas*, p. 163. Reprinted with permission.

[16] A summary of the various programs in operation in 1962 can be found in U.S., Department of Health, Education, and Welfare, Office of Education, *Programs for Educationally Disadvantaged* (Washington: U.S. Government Printing Office, 1962).

upon education as an implement of change constitute important environ- mental changes which took place between the school-aid fight in 1961 and the passage of the federal aid bill in 1965. The manner in which this development was utilized by the proponents of the aid in 1965 will be illustrated below. However, before beginning that discussion, it is neces- sary to review the educational changes that resulted from metropoli- tanism and from the civil rights movement since these factors contributed additional new environmental inputs.

METROPOLITANISM AND CITY SCHOOLS

The renewed interest in alleviating poverty and its implications for education occurred almost simultaneously with the recognition of another set of social patterns that also produced important consequences for the education function. These patterns include the concurrent shift of people, jobs, and economic activities from rural to urban and from city to sub- urban areas of the nation. This total process and its various social, economic, and political concomitants have been designated as metropoli- tanization.[17] It is important to note that in contrast to the term urbaniza- tion, which basically refers to the growth of relatively large, densely populated, nonfarm centers (cities) and all of the accompanying con- ditions, the concept of metropolitanization stresses the spill-over of urban type populations and activities beyond the governmental boundaries of cities into the surrounding area. This latter process is not new; in fact, it began at a noticeable pace in the last half of the nineteenth century.[18] However, its reacceleration occurred in the post-World War II period, as is clear from the data presented in Table 3.

The statistics included in this table represent an attempt to summarize three relevant population trends: (1) the population within metropolitan areas has increased since 1900 at a more rapid rate than the United States population in general; (2) the proportion of the United States population living within metropolitan areas has increased since 1900 and is now 65 per cent of the total; and (3) the proportion of the population within metropolitan areas living outside the central cities has increased con- siderably since 1940, when it was at approximately the same level that it was at the turn of the century.

[17] Much recent literature deals with this topic. For good general accounts see Roscoe Martin and Douglas Price, *The Metropolis and Its Problems* (Syracuse: Maxwell Graduate School, Syracuse University, 1960); Scott Greer, *The Emerging City: Myth and Reality* (New York: The Free Press, 1962); James Bollens and Henry Schmandt, *The Metropolis* (New York: Harper and Row, 1965).

[18] See Adna F. Weber, *The Growth of the Cities in the Nineteenth Century* (New York: The Macmillan Company, 1899), and Blake McKelvey, *The Urbanization of America, 1860–1915* (New Brunswick: Rutgers University Press, 1963), particularly pp. 232–38.

The latter development, in terms of this study, is most significant since it hints at an important population characteristic of the metropolitan process: the decentralization of population from the central city to areas outside the central city. The trend is illustrated more clearly and specifically in Table 4, which shows the shift in population in both sectors of the fifteen largest metropolitan areas for the decade 1950–60. The central

TABLE 3

POPULATION GROWTH IN THE UNITED STATES IN METROPOLITAN AREAS
AND DISTRIBUTION WITHIN METROPOLITAN AREAS, 1900–65
(Conterminous United States)

	United States		SMSA		SMSA as % of Total Population	% of SMSA Population Outside Central Cities
	Population (million)	% Increase by Decade	Population (million)	% Increase by Decade		
1900	75.995	—	31.836	—	41.9	37.8
1910	91.972	21.0	42.012	32.0	45.7	35.4
1920	105.711	14.9	52.508	25.0	49.7	34.0
1930	122.775	16.1	66.712	27.1	54.3	35.4
1940	131.669	7.2	72.576	8.8	55.1	37.3
1950	150.597	14.5	88.964	22.6	59.0	41.3
1960	178.464	18.4	112.385	26.3	63.0	48.6
1965	192.185	—	123.813	—	65.0	51.9

SOURCE: U.S., Bureau of the Census, *U.S. Census of Population: 1960 Selected Area Reports, Standard Metropolitan Statistical Areas,* and *Current Population Reports,* Series P-20, No. 151, April 19, 1966.

cities of these metropolitan areas, with the exception of Milwaukee, Los Angeles, and the southern cities, all experienced a decline in population during the ten-year period while the areas outside these central cities all had substantial population increases. Although the figures are for only 15 of the 212 metropolitan areas in 1960, they are generally representative of national patterns. The southern and western metropolitan areas have experienced population growth in both the central city and outside the central city; however, in the other sections of the country the large central cities have tended to either remain at their 1950 population level or lose, while their suburban areas have gained, population.[19]

These population trends alone carry implications for education. The rapid increase of population in the area outside central cities, particularly

[19] For a discussion of these regional differences see Alan K. Campbell and Seymour Sacks, *Metropolitan America: Fiscal Patterns and Governmental Systems* (forthcoming publication, The Free Press, 1967).

married couples with young children, put a tremendous strain on the educational facilities available in these areas and was responsible, in part, for the large capital expenditures of suburban school districts during the 1950's. However, these basic population trends take on even greater significance for the education function when they are examined in rela-

TABLE 4

POPULATION GROWTH IN CENTRAL CITY AND OUTSIDE CENTRAL CITY AREAS
FOR FIFTEEN LARGEST SMSA'S, 1950–60

	Central City		Outside Central City	
	1960 Population (million)	% Increase Since 1950	1960 Population (million)	% Increase Since 1950
New York	7.781	− 1.4	2.912	75.0
Chicago	3.550	− 1.9	2.670	71.5
Los Angeles[a]	2.823	27.1	3.919	82.6
Philadelphia	2.002	− 3.3	2.340	46.3
Detroit	1.670	− 9.7	2.092	79.3
Baltimore	.939	− 1.1	.787	72.4
Houston	.938	57.4	.304	44.8
Cleveland	.876	− 4.2	.920	67.2
Washington	.763	− 4.8	.661	87.0
St. Louis	.750	−12.5	1.310	51.9
Milwaukee	.741	16.3	.452	41.7
San Francisco[b]	1.159	− 4.5	1.075	55.0
Boston	.697	−13.0	1.892	17.6
Dallas	.679	56.4	.403	30.7
New Orleans	.627	10.0	.240	109.6
United States (all SMSA's)	58.004	10.7	54.880	48.6

[a] Includes Long Beach.
[b] Includes Oakland.
SOURCE: U.S., Bureau of the Census, *U.S. Census of Population: 1960,* Vol. I, *Characteristics of the Population,* Part A, Number of Inhabitants, Table 33.

tion to such factors as race, income, and educational attainment. Examined in these terms, it becomes apparent that the redistribution of population within metropolitan areas has not occurred on a random basis. The population shift is not only a matter of number of people, it also involves a sorting-out process. In general, it is the poor, less-educated, nonwhite Americans who tend to remain in the central city and the higher-income, better-educated whites who tend to move out, although this description must be qualified somewhat in terms of the metropolitan area's size and its regional location in the country. The larger the metropolitan area, however, the more accurate is this description.

Table 5 illustrates this point, that population redistribution has not been on a random basis, in terms of the emerging racial composition of large central cities. The table indicates that all of the largest central cities, regardless of whether or not they lost population since 1950, had a considerable increase in Negro population.[20] In addition, eleven out of the

TABLE 5
WHITE AND NEGRO POPULATION CHANGES IN FIFTEEN
LARGEST CITIES, 1950–60

	White Population		Negro Population		
	1960 (million)	% Change Since 1950	1960 (million)	% Change Since 1950	% of 1960 Total
New York	6.641	− 6.7	1.088	45.5	14.0
Chicago	2.713	−12.8	.813	65.1	22.9
Los Angeles[a]	2.391	19.4	.344	96.3	12.2
Philadelphia	1.407	−13.3	.529	40.7	26.4
Detroit	1.183	−23.5	.482	60.5	28.9
Baltimore	.611	−15.6	.326	44.6	34.7
Houston	.721	53.1	.215	72.4	22.9
Cleveland	.623	−18.6	.251	69.6	28.6
Washington	.345	−33.3	.412	46.6	53.9
St. Louis	.534	−24.0	.214	39.4	28.6
Milwaukee	.676	9.9	.062	186.9	8.4
San Francisco[b]	.875	−14.4	.158	73.5	14.3
Boston	.629	−17.1	.063	57.9	9.1
Dallas	.548	45.5	.129	126.9	19.0
New Orleans	.393	1.2	.234	28.5	37.2
All Central Cities	47.575	4.7	9.704	50.3	16.8

a Includes Long Beach.

b Includes Oakland.

SOURCE: U.S., Bureau of the Census, *U.S. Census of Population: 1960, Selected Area Reports, Standard Metropolitan Statistical Areas,* Table 1.

fifteen cities underwent a simultaneous loss of white population. Again, regional differences exist; but, as the total line in the table shows, central cities in general are becoming increasingly inhabited by Negroes.

The decrease in whites, who are generally middle class in their social and economic characteristics, and the increase in Negroes, who are less affluent economically, present central cities with a number of general

[20] This is not a new pattern; for a discussion of the 1940–50 decade see Morton Grodzins, *The Metropolitan Area as a Racial Problem* (Pittsburgh: University of Pittsburgh Press, 1958).

problems and with some specific educational problems.[21] For example, if low income is related to educational achievement, and there is considerable evidence that it is, then the fact that central cities are becoming increasingly inhabited by Negroes has an important impact on the school system due to, among other things, the income characteristics of Negroes.[22]

Negroes earn less than whites in the United States. Specifically, the median income for all white income earners in 1959 was $3,027 per year compared to $1,519 for all Negro earners—about 50 per cent of the white income. More recent data indicate that the relative levels have not changed. In 1963 white male workers fourteen years and older earned $4,816 in contrast to $2,444 for Negro male workers, again about a 50 per cent difference.[23]

These income differences are reflected in data which compare the proportion of familes earning less than $3,000 on a central city–outside central city basis. Central cities in general have a larger percentage of such families than do their suburban areas—18 per cent to 12 per cent, respectively. Even more significant, given the population trends discussed above, is the fact that the population of central city nonwhites with incomes under $3,000 is more than double the aggregate white proportion—14 per cent compared to 36 per cent.[24] Consequently, if present population shifts continue, and there is little evidence that they will not, it is clear that many central cities will become the principal location of the poverty groups discussed above.

An examination of the data presented in Table 6 suggests another future characteristic of large central cities. It indicates that the 1960 proportion of the central city population twenty-five years and older with at least four years of high school was less than 40 per cent while in urban fringe communities the comparable figure was 52 per cent.[25] The last

[21] For a comparison of relevant differences see U.S., Department of Labor, *The Economic Situation of Negroes in the United States* (Washington: U.S. Government Printing Office, 1962); U.S., Bureau of the Census, *Current Population Reports,* Series P-20, No. 142, "Negro Population: March 1965," (Washington: U.S. Government Printing Office, 1965); and U.S., Department of Labor, *The Negro Family: The Case for National Action* (Washington: U.S. Government Printing Office, 1965).

[22] See Sexton, *Education and Income;* James *et al., Wealth, Expenditures, and Decision-Making for Education;* and Burkhead, *Input and Output in Large-City High Schools.*

[23] U.S., Bureau of the Census, "Negro Population: March, 1965," and U.S., Department of Labor, *The Negro Family: The Case for National Action.*

[24] Negroes constitute 92 per cent of nonwhites in the United States; thus the words are used interchangeably in this study.

[25] Urban fringe is that portion of the outside central city area which is most "thickly settled" according to criteria established by the Census Bureau.

column in this table shows that this difference is likely to become even greater as the nonwhite proportion of the cities' population increases. These latter figures seem to indicate that approximately 70 per cent of nonwhite central city students have parents with less than a high school education. Indeed, about 61 per cent of Negroes twenty-five years old and over had no more than eight years of schooling in 1960.

TABLE 6

EDUCATIONAL ATTAINMENT OF PERSONS TWENTY-FIVE YEARS OR OLDER IN FIFTEEN URBANIZED AREAS, BY RESIDENCE, BY COLOR, 1960

Urbanized Area	Percentage with 4 Years of High School or More		
	Central City	Urban Fringe	Central City Nonwhites
New York	36.4	48.7	31.2
Chicago	35.3	53.9	27.3
Los Angeles	53.4	53.4	43.6
Philadelphia	30.7	48.0	23.6
Detroit	34.4	47.5	26.5
Baltimore	28.2	42.3	19.7
Houston	45.2	50.1	26.2
Cleveland	30.1	55.5	28.1
Washington	47.8	67.5	33.5
St. Louis	26.3	43.3	20.2
Milwaukee	39.7	54.4	26.0
San Francisco	49.4	57.9	39.1
Boston	44.6	55.8	36.2
Dallas	48.9	56.4	25.2
New Orleans	33.3	44.6	15.0
Mean	38.4	52.0	28.3

SOURCE: Computed from U.S., Bureau of the Census, *U.S. Census of Population: 1960, General Social and Economic Characteristics* (Washington: U.S. Government Printing Office, 1961) and *U.S. Census of Population and Housing: 1960, Census Tracts.*

These income and educational characteristics of adult Negroes have several implications for school-age Negroes. Coming from families with low income and educational levels, they are less likely than the average middle-class white pupil to be exposed to an environment that has material objects such as magazines, books, records, and study areas which aid a student's school performance or that has a value structure which stresses the importance of educational achievement. As is indicated by the material in Table 7, students with such a background make up a considerable proportion of the school population in large cities. In many respects they constitute the basic problem confronting these school districts because they require special educational services that central city school districts cannot support given their declining fiscal resources.[26] If the present population trends continue and if white families remaining in the central city send their children to private schools in increasing numbers, as they presently are, then other central city school districts may be confronted with a school population that is over 75 per cent nonwhite, as is now the case in Washington, D.C., and may encounter the problems that accompany such a school population.

TABLE 7

PERCENTAGE NONWHITE POPULATION CONTRASTED WITH PERCENTAGE NONWHITE
SCHOOL ENROLLMENT FOR FIFTEEN LARGEST CITIES, 1960

	% Nonwhite of Total Population	% Nonwhite of School Population
New York	14.0	22.0
Chicago	22.9	39.8
Los Angeles	12.2	20.5
Philadelphia	26.4	46.7
Detroit	28.9	42.9
Baltimore	34.7	50.1
Houston	22.9	30.2
Cleveland	28.6	46.1
Washington	53.9	77.5
St. Louis	28.6	48.8
Milwaukee	8.4	16.2
San Francisco	14.3	30.5
Boston	9.1	16.4
Dallas	19.0	26.0
New Orleans	37.2	55.4

SOURCE: U.S., Bureau of the Census, *U.S. Census of Population: 1960, Selected Area Reports, Standard Metropolitan Statistical Areas,* and *General Social and Economic Characteristics: 1960.*

This brief discussion has attempted to outline some of the salient aspects of postwar metropolitanization that are most relevant to the educational conditions existing in large cities. It is not suggested that the process of metropolitanism and its consequences are unique to the 1961–65 period, but that those aspects which were identified as being most pertinent to urban education became particularly visible in the mid-1960's. The proponents of federal aid to education explicitly related these factors to that issue during the 1965 congressional hearings. Several events apparently stimulated the increased recognition of these conditions.

[26] For a discussion of this point see Alan K. Campbell and Philip Meranto, "The Metropolitan Education Dilemma: Matching Resources to Needs," *Urban Affairs Quarterly,* September, 1966.

As noted earlier, the publication of Harrington's volume, *The Other America,* played an important role in stirring renewed interest in alleviating American poverty. A book written by James B. Conant in 1961, entitled *Slums and Suburbs,* performed a similar function by calling attention to the status of large-city education systems. In this slim but widely referred to volume, Conant contrasts the dichotomous characteristics of public schools in what he designates as "city slums and wealthy suburbs." He argues that:

> [W]e are allowing social dynamite to accumulate in our large cities. . . . The building up of a mass of unemployed and frustrated Negro youth in congested areas of a city is a social phenomenon that may be compared to the piling up of inflammable material in an empty building in a city block. Potentialities for trouble—indeed possibilities of disaster—are surely there.[27]

This view is based upon a number of characteristics which Conant attributes to schools in large central cities. He points out that the large northern cities are being inhabited increasingly by low income and "inadequately" educated Negroes, many of whom have recently moved from the rural sections of the South. Their children, who are in need of special educational training and services because of their background, are becoming a larger and larger proportion of the school population in these cities. This increase in need has put the city schools at a disadvantage because of the financial condition of cities relative to their suburban areas. Conant argues that, while wealthy suburban school districts can afford to support per pupil expenditures of $1,000 per year, big-city school districts, with their needy student populations, spend less than half that amount. In addition, suburban districts generally have spacious and well-equipped modern school plants manned by as many as 70 professionals per 1,000 pupils in contrast to city slum schools which often are overcrowded, dilapidated structures staffed by 40 or fewer professionals per 1,000 pupils.[28]

Conant admits that he selected extreme cases and somewhat over-simplified comparisons to illustrate his point. But, significantly, his depiction of the educational problems in city schools as contrasted to those in suburban schools was accurate enough to gain widespread attention and comment. While this book was in the public eye, another set of circumstances simultaneously gained momentum and apparently did much to attract public attention to the educational situation in

[27] James B. Conant, *Slums and Suburbs: A Commentary on Schools in Metropolitan Areas* (New York: New American Library, 1961), pp. 10, 24.
[28] *Ibid.,* pp. 11–12.

large cities; it was the accelerated pace of the civil rights movement and its role in highlighting the predicament of urban schools and Negroes in American society.

THE NEW THRUST OF CIVIL RIGHTS

The plight of the American Negro has been related too well and too often by others to be repeated profitably here. Rather than reiterating the historical factors that have contributed to the status accorded to Negroes in the United States and the earlier attempts made to improve their situation, this section focuses on some of the more recent efforts made to grant Negroes an equal opportunity to take their rightful part in the social, economic, and political life of the society.

It is, of course, difficult to date with any certainty the beginning of the current phase of the civil rights movement, but surely two events of the mid-1950's gave an important impetus to the recent struggle. The first was the historic decision rendered by the United States Supreme Court on May 18, 1954, in the case of *Brown* v. *Board of Education of Topeka*. Writing for a unanimous court, Chief Justice Earl Warren stated that ". . . in the field of public education the doctrine of 'separate but equal' has no place. Separate educational facilities are inherently unequal."[29] Although the Court's implementing decree did not command the immediate admission of Negro pupils to schools from which they had been barred previously, it did state that the transition to a racially non-discriminatory school system should be accomplished "with all deliberate speed." Certainly many proponents of school desegregation are not pleased with its pace, particularly in the deep South where little more than 2 per cent of all Negro students are attending schools with whites. Still, the *Brown* v. *Board of Education* decision established an important principle in the field of civil rights and provided renewed energy for civil rights advocates.[30]

In the winter of 1955–56 a second event gave the civil rights movement an additional injection. Led by the young Baptist minister, Martin Luther King, Jr., who preached the strength of nonviolent resistance, the Negroes of Montgomery, Alabama, staged a bus boycott that gained national attention. King and his organization, the Southern Christian Leadership Conference, stressed the strategy of mass, but peaceful, action which brought Negroes into the streets to press their case for equality. In contrast to the methods of such organizations as the National Associa-

---

[29] Quoted in U.S., Commission on Civil Rights, *Freedom to the Free* (Washington: U.S. Government Printing Office, 1963), p. 147.

[30] See Bayard Rustin, "From Protest to Politics: The Future of the Civil Rights Movement," in Louis A. Ferman *et al., Poverty in America*, pp. 457–70.

tion for the Advancement of Colored People, which generally pursued objectives through the courts or through quiet negotiation, the new approach began the mode of involving large numbers of Negroes in demonstrations.

Further momentum was gained in the civil rights movement in February, 1960, when four Negro students at the Agricultural and Technical College in Greensboro, North Carolina, sat down at a lunch counter and were denied service. They decided to stay in their seats until the diner closed, thus initiating the "sit-in" and bringing into prominence another civil rights organization, the Congress of Racial Equality. The sit-ins eventually led to kneel-ins, pray-ins, stall-ins, and other forms of nonviolent protest. By the spring of 1961, Negroes and whites rode together through the South on "Freedom Buses," demanding their legal rights to share alike in the restaurants, waiting rooms, and rest rooms at interstate rail and bus terminals.[31]

Intensity of action reached an all-time high during April and May of 1963 in Birmingham, Alabama. Described by King as "the most thoroughly segregated big city in the U.S.," Birmingham became the target for a mass, nonviolent campaign to end discrimination in restaurants, shops, and employment. Marchers met with an ardent advocate of segregation in Police Commissioner Eugene "Bull" Connor who secured an injunction against the march. Connor and his deputies met the marchers daily and arrested hundreds of them. King himself was jailed on Good Friday, April 12; by Easter Sunday the happenings in Birmingham became the focus of national attention. During the first week of May, daily newspapers and evening television programs showed the marchers, including many women and children, being snapped at by police dogs and thrashed by powerful fire hoses. The police dogs and fire hoses of Birmingham became, as Theodore White has suggested, the symbols of the American Negro revolution and, in a sense, the symbols that pricked the conscience of the nation.[32] Indeed, it is reported that President Kennedy often said, "The civil rights movement should thank God for Bull Connor. He helped it as much as Abraham Lincoln."[33]

Although the new push for civil rights was initiated in the South, it gained sufficient momentum to make the issues equally important and dynamic in the northern and western urban centers. The social and

[31] The Interstate Commerce Commission had ruled in 1955 that the segregation of interstate transportation facilities was illegal.

[32] Theodore H. White, *The Making of the President, 1964* (New York: Atheneum Publishers, 1965). See pp. 170–99 and 232–54 for an interpretation of the impact of the civil rights movements on national presidential politics.

[33] Quoted in Theodore C. Sorensen, *Kennedy* (New York: Harper and Row, 1965), p. 489.

economic problems confronting Negroes in the major central cities seemed to become more conspicuous. Repeatedly, the question was raised concerning the extent to which the schools were perpetuating, instead of reducing, the problem.

Evidently, some Negroes and Negro organizations felt that the schools were doing more to perpetuate the problems than to solve them. In 1964, for example, a series of school boycotts were conducted by Negroes in New York City, Chicago, and several other cities. Protesting the existence and spread of what has come to be called *de facto* school segregation, the boycotters argued that more and more Negro students were being forced to attend schools exclusively or predominantly populated by Negroes.[34] Although some acknowledged that the increase in *de facto* segregation was related to the changing population composition of the cities, the protesters stressed that the increase was due to the past gerrymandering of school district lines by school officials and the present lack of redistricting or other corrective methods which would result in racially balanced schools. In addition, they claimed that schools with large nonwhite student bodies were generally second-rate; such schools were more likely than "white" schools to be overcrowded, old, dilapidated, and lacking in educational equipment. More importantly, these schools tended to be staffed by less qualified teachers, many of whom are substitutes seldom willing to go to or remain in a "slum" school if they can avoid it. It was argued that Negro pupils, as a result of these factors, received less than an equal opportunity to achieve an adequate education. Not believing that predominantly nonwhite schools will or can be upgraded, Negro spokesmen have continued to press for integrated schools, arguing that this is the only means to ensure quality education for Negro youngsters.[35]

The validity of the criticisms leveled at the schools by protesters and

[34] For an analysis of the New York boycotts, see Bert E. Swanson, *School Integration Controversies in New York City* (Washington, D.C.: Office of Education, Cooperative Research Project No. 2857, 1965). See also Robert L. Crain, *School Desegregation in the North* (Chicago: National Opinion Research Center, 1966), for a discussion of the politics of school integration in eight large cities.

[35] Literature on this general issue is voluminous. For some selected discussions see Nathan Glazer, "Is Integration Possible in the New York City Schools?" *Commentary*, September, 1960; Will Maslow, "De Facto Public School Segregation," *Villanova Law Review*, Spring, 1961; Daniel Levine, "City Schools Today: Too Late with Too Little," *Phi Delta Kappan*, Spring, 1961; Jeremy Larner, "The New York School Crisis," *Dissent*, Spring, 1964; Charles E. Silberman, *Crisis in Black and White* (New York: Random House, 1964), Chapter 9, "The Negro and the School"; and Martin Mayer, "Close to Midnight for the New York Schools," *The New York Times Magazine*, May 2, 1965.

the usefulness of the strategies they have utilized to pursue their goals are complex issues which will not be explored here. More central to the concern of this study is the fact that all of the boycotts, demonstrations, public meetings, newspaper articles, books, and television broadcasts that have dealt with these issues have performed the function of focusing public attention and concern on the circumstances of central city schools.

Demonstrations and publicity, in both the southern and northern regions of the country, have made the current civil rights movement one of the central forces of social change in contemporary America. In addition to its general influence, a strengthened civil rights movement has had an important bearing on the topic of this study in two specific ways: (1) it promoted the enactment of the Civil Rights Act of 1964, which eventually undercut an issue that previously had complicated the passage of federal aid to education bills; (2) it called renewed attention to the relative circumstances of Negroes in America, particularly in relation to the educational opportunities available to Negro youngsters in the cities.

The initial action pressing for additional civil rights legislation began during the Kennedy administration. President John F. Kennedy, after much consultation with various parties and deep consideration of the possible influence on the enactment of other key programs, sent his civil rights bill to Congress on June 19, 1963.[36] Reiterating statistics he had used in his opening debate with presidential candidate Richard Nixon and in his civil rights message of February, 1963, the President noted:

> The Negro baby born in America today, regardless of the section of the nation in which he is born, has about one-half as much chance of completing high school as a white baby born in the same place on the same day, one-third as much chance of completing college, one-third as much chance of becoming a professional man, twice as much chance of becoming unemployed, about one-seventh as much chance of earning $10,000 a year, a life expectancy which is seven years shorter, and the prospects of earning only one-half as much.[37]

Among other things, the proposed legislation called for a variety of reformulations in the voting rights laws, governmental authority to file

[36] For insightful accounts concerning the political issues surrounding civil rights, the type of bill proposed, and its timing, see Sorensen, *Kennedy*, pp. 470–506, and Arthur M. Schlesinger, Jr., *A Thousand Days: John F. Kennedy in the White House* (Boston: Houghton Mifflin Company, 1965), pp. 924-77.

[37] Quoted in Sorensen, *Kennedy*, p. 472.

suit to desegregate public accommodations, a provision which would supply the Attorney General the power to initiate school desegregation suits, additional programs to assure fair employment, and a provision authorizing the federal government to withhold funds for programs in which discrimination was practiced.

During his first appearance before the United States Congress following the assassination of President Kennedy, President Johnson urged "the earliest possible passage of the civil rights bill for which he [Kennedy had] fought so long." The bill was passed in the House of Representatives by a two-to-one margin in February, 1964. After a filibuster of almost three months, the Senate took the unprecedented step of voting to curtail a filibuster against civil rights legislation. The Senate bill was altered to place more stress on local enforcement, and the House accepted the bill as modified by the Senate. Before a nation-wide television audience on July 2, 1964, Johnson signed the bill into law.

Under Title VI of the 1964 Civil Rights Act no program or activity receiving federal assistance may discriminate against persons because of race, color, or national origin. If a federal agency finds such practices exist and if these practices are not voluntarily terminated, the agency is authorized to halt the distribution of funds to the unit involved after providing an opportunity for a hearing and after giving the appropriate legislative committees thirty days' notice.

Six months later, when Congress began hearings on the Education Act of 1965, the inclusion of Title VI in the civil rights legislation generally eliminated from the sphere of discussion a controversial issue—the granting of federal aid to segregated education systems—which had in recent years been one of the key factors hindering the creation of a solid coalition of federal aid proponents.

Since 1950 the National Association for the Advancement of Colored People (NAACP), which has always supported federal aid for education, has insisted that any aid-to-education program include a stipulation barring federal funds to segregated schools.[38] Testifying before the House Subcommittee on Education in 1961, Clarence Mitchell, director of the Washington Bureau of the NAACP, made it clear that this position was not subject to compromise when he stated:

> We shall never cease to resist the dishonest and undemocratic idea that the taxpayers of all the States should be called upon to build seg-

---

[38] Prior to 1950 the NAACP had stressed the equal distribution of funds among schools. See Munger and Fenno, *National Politics and Federal Aid to Education,* pp. 65–72.

regated schools in a few states; nor shall we be silent when such proposals are made.[39]

Other advocates of federal aid, to the dismay of the NAACP, have been more willing on occasion to concede the point in their enthusiasm to attract southern support for school-aid bills. Although condemning segregation in schools, many of the groups (such as the National Education Association and the AFL-CIO) have opposed, at one time or another, an anti-segregation amendment to pending bills. Even Negro congressmen have split previously on the issue; Representative Adam Clayton Powell has often introduced, or threatened to introduce, such an amendment and has been supported by Representative Charles Diggs of Detroit but opposed by Representative William Dawson of Chicago.[40]

However, the existence of the Civil Rights Act of 1964 during the 1965 congressional hearings and floor debates on aid to education meant that dissension resulting from the segregation issue was no longer a potential threat to the creation of a cohesive proponent coalition. It also eliminated the possibility of non-southern opponents of aid voting for the inclusion of a segregation amendment, then voting against the bill on a final roll call, as was the case in 1956 and 1960. Consequently, the civil rights legislation of 1964 represents an excellent example of how a previous output of the political system may have a feedback effect on the current political process.

THE RATIONALE FOR FEDERAL AID TO EDUCATION: 1965 VERSION

In this review of poverty, metropolitanism, and civil rights an attempt has been made to specify the nature of three environmental changes which occurred in American society during the early 1960's. The remaining task is twofold: to demonstrate how these environmental changes were utilized by the proponents of school aid in 1965 in constructing their new argument for federal support of education and to make some assessment of the effectiveness of this approach in promoting the passage of the 1965 legislation.

The first public hint concerning the kind of federal aid to education program that would be presented for consideration to the Eighty-ninth Congress was given by President Johnson in his State of the Union Message on January 4, 1965. Reviewing the national agenda, the President stated: "I propose we begin a program in education to insure every American child the fullest development of his mind and skills."

[39] House Committee on Education and Labor, *Federal Aid to Schools,* p. 666.
[40] James Q. Wilson, *Negro Politics: The Search for Leadership* (New York: The Free Press, 1960), pp. 114–15.

Later in the message he elaborated slightly by saying: "For the primary and secondary school years we will aid public schools serving low-income families and assist students in both public and private schools."[41]

The premises and dimensions of the elementary and secondary program were put forth more explicitly by the President in his education message to the Congress on January 12, 1965. After reviewing American accomplishments in the field of education and the nation's dependence on a strong educational system, the President declared, "There is a darker side to education in America." He included in this view the student dropout rate, the growing unemployment of young people with an eighth grade education or less, the proportion of students not able to pursue a higher education, the growth of enrollment at the elementary and secondary level, and the need for facilities to meet this growth. Referring to education as "the No. 1 business of the American people," he outlined his programs.

In the section devoted to elementary and secondary education he noted that, in the past, six or seven years of schooling did not seriously restrict an individual's opportunities; "but, today, lack of formal education is likely to mean low wages, frequent unemployment, and a home in an urban or rural slum."

The President continued his message by describing the relationship between a deficient education and poverty:

> Poverty has many roots, but the taproot is ignorance: Poverty is the lot of two-thirds of the families in which the family head has had 9 years or less of schooling.
> Twenty percent of the youth aged 19 to 24 with an eighth-grade education or less are unemployed—four times the national average.[42]

He stressed the point that poverty is not evenly distributed throughout the nation, thus it presents special educational problems for areas with disproportionate levels of poverty. Here the linkage was made between poverty and cities. The pattern was summarized by the President in the following terms:

> The burden on the Nation's schools is not evenly distributed. Low-income families are heavily concentrated in particular urban neighborhoods or rural areas. Faced with the largest educational needs, many of these school districts have inadequate financial resources. This imbalance has been increased by the movement of high income families

[41] U.S., Senate, Committee on Labor and Public Welfare, *Elementary and Secondary Education Act of 1965: Background Material with Related Presidential Recommendations,* 89th Cong., 1st Sess., 1965, pp. 5, 7.
[42] *Ibid.,* p. 14.

from the center of cities to the suburbs—and their replacement by low-income families from rural areas.

Despite a massive effort, our big cities generally spend only about two thirds as much per pupil as their adjacent suburbs.

In our 15 largest cities, 60 percent of the 10th grade students from poverty neighborhoods drop out before finishing high school.

This is a national problem. Federal action is needed to assist the States and localities in bringing the full benefits of education to children of low-income families.[43]

The recommended national response to these conditions was Title I of the Elementary and Secondary Education Act of 1965. As noted previously, this is the key title of the act. It provides federal funds to school districts based on the total number of five- to seventeen-year-old children in the district from families with annual incomes below $2,000 and from families with higher incomes as a consequence of aid-to-dependent-children relief payments multiplied by 50 per cent of the average per-pupil expenditure in the state during the school year 1963–64.

In order to receive the funds allocated to it on the basis of this formula, a school district must take an assessment of the educational needs of low-income students in both public and private schools in its area and design special programs to assist these students. Once the plans are formulated, they are submitted to the state department of education for review; if the state approves the plans, the funds authorized are forwarded to the local school district. The state education department is responsible for seeing that the plans are carried out and for providing the federal Office of Education with evaluative reports.

In addition to recommending a program of assistance to schools serving children of low-income families, the President also recommended a program to authorize grants to assist states in purchasing books for school libraries (Title II); a proposal to provide federal funds for the establishment of supplementary education centers and services within communities (Title III); the creation, under the Cooperative Research Act, of regional educational laboratories to undertake research, train teachers, and implement tested research findings (Title IV); and a program to provide federal assistance to strengthen state education departments (Title V).[44]

Hearings on the administration's bill were held before the respective congressional committees during the last week of January and the first

---

[43] *Ibid.*, pp. 14–15.
[44] More will be said about these other titles of the act as they relate to the political issues that are discussed in Chapters III and IV.

week of February, 1965. The leading administration witnesses were, of course, Secretary of Health, Education, and Welfare Anthony J. Celebrezze and Commissioner of Education Francis Keppel.

Speaking before the House Subcommittee on Education on January 22, Secretary Celebrezze reviewed the President's request and described it as "something new and different in magnitude, in concept and in direction. . . . It is a major innovation from Federal proposals and policies in recent decades, particularly with respect to elementary and secondary education."[45] Quoting the President's remarks on poverty in America, the Secretary noted: "The President's program as embodied in H.R. 2362 is designed to break this cycle which has been running on from generation to generation in this most affluent period of our history."

In a similar fashion to the President's education message, the Secretary sketched the relationships among poor education and poverty, unemployment, delinquency, and crime. He continued by stressing the seriousness of the dropout problem and the concentration of poverty in the cities and rural areas.

> The cause of these dropouts, and the despair and disillusionment that characterize them, is not so much that students have failed education as that education, as they have found it, has far too often failed them.
>
> Education's deficiencies, we have come to recognize, are nowhere more marked than in the poverty of the schools that serve the children of the poor—in the heart of our great cities and in many rural communities. In the case of these cities and communities, poverty reduces local resources to the peril point. Because the tax base is low, funds for education are inadequate and the schools and the children suffer.[46]

Commissioner Keppel's testimony emphasized the correlations among poverty, undereducation, unemployment, and the lack of financial resources of cities and rural areas to meet their educational needs. Referring to the President's proposal to meet these problems, he said:

> The new program dramatically parts company with education proposals and policies of the past. . . . It provides aid to students in elementary and secondary schools to a larger degree than ever before proposed. It gives special and long-needed attention to the education of the children of the poor who need the best our schools can give and who usually have received the worst. . . . It commits education to end the paralysis that poverty breeds, a paralysis that is chronic and contagious and runs on from generation to generation.[47]

[45] U.S., House, Committee on Education and Labor, *Aid to Elementary and Secondary Education*, 89th Cong., 1st Sess., 1965, p. 65.
[46] *Ibid.*, p. 66.
[47] *Ibid.*, p. 83.

He supported his testimony by submitting the partial results of several studies that indicated the relationship between income and educational attainment. He cited a study of Tucson, Arizona, in which the forty-five census tracts of the city were divided into five major groups on the basis of proximity and similarity of income, educational achievement, and housing conditions. As Table 8 indicates, the census groups with the lowest family income had the lowest percentage of high school graduates and the highest dropouts rates.

TABLE 8

DROPOUT AND GRADUATION RATES IN TUCSON PUBLIC HIGH SCHOOLS, 1960–61, AND SOCIOECONOMIC DATA BY GROUPS OF CENSUS TRACTS, 1960

Census Group	Total Population	Median Years of School	Median Income	% Drop-outs	% Graduates
I	28,195	8.4	$3,669	17.1	37
II	44,052	10.2	4,726	10.5	58
III	39,996	11.8	5,308	10.4	75
IV	47,863	12.3	5,873	7.0	70
V	80,367	12.6	6,804	3.7	90

Supplementing the development of the bill's rationale as constructed by the President, Secretary Celebrezze, and Commissioner Keppel was the testimony of large-city school superintendents. Superintendents representing fourteen large cities[48] were divided into two groups: one to appear before the House committee, the other before the Senate. Each superintendent briefly discussed the kinds of problems confronting large-city school systems. They usually illustrated their points with references to conditions in their own districts and commented on how the legislation under review would aid in mitigating some of the problems.

The summary statement presented by Dr. Benjamin C. Willis, superintendent of Chicago schools and moderator of the panel appearing before the Senate, is typical of the case presented by the large-city representatives before the committee members. He stated:

> To summarize, I would say that the great cities of America are confronted by unique educational problems:

[48] The cities included were Baltimore, Boston, Buffalo, Chicago, Cleveland, Detroit, Houston, Los Angeles, Milwaukee, New York City, Philadelphia, Pittsburgh, San Francisco, and St. Louis. They represented 27 million people and about 11 per cent of all public school students. It is of interest to note the cities voted overwhelmingly Democratic in the 1964 presidential election; the largest Republican proportion, 35.4 per cent, was recorded in Los Angeles.

(1) Well-educated and highly skilled people are moving out of the city.

(2) Their places are being taken by large families from the rural South.

(3) In the midst of rapidly developing technological advances, the adults among the newcomers have little education and limited vocational skills.

(4) The children, retarded in academic achievement, and lacking in motivation for school, require specialized programs of education if they are to overcome the disadvantages imposed upon them by their limited backgrounds.

(5) Programs to meet the needs of disadvantaged children have been successfully demonstrated in each of the great cities but these cannot be extended to serve all of the children in need because of lack of financial resources.

(6) Local support of education comes largely from taxes on property; 12 cities pay well over 60 percent of the cost of operating their schools from local taxes.

(7) By 1965 enrollments in the schools of the great cities will have increased 48.6 percent over 1950, and these enrollments include large numbers of pupils requiring costly specialized programs.

(8) Site and construction costs are considerably higher in the large cities than in smaller communities.

(9) A large portion of the tax dollar in the great cities is required for nonschool governmental services.

(10) In the face of increased need for financial resources, there is a smaller assessable tax base behind each child in the schools in the great cities than ever before.

(11) The sharing of taxes from other sources and from other levels of government is required in order for the great cities to provide opportunities for their children, each in accordance with his need.[49]

More testimony easily could be included to denote the kind of rationale used to support the request for federal aid for elementary and secondary education in 1965, but certainly the point is already obvious. The argument was clearly presented in terms of poverty and the consequences of metropolitanism, thus departing considerably from past approaches.

CONCLUSIONS

The remaining question is how effective was the new approach in influencing congressmen to support the legislation. Any attempt to

[49] Senate Committee on Labor and Public Welfare, *Elementary and Secondary Education Act of 1965*, 89th Cong. 1st Sess., pp. 1210–11.

answer this question immediately encounters the difficulty of isolating the influence of the bill's rationale from other factors that congressmen consider before casting their votes, such as the preferences of their party leaders, their constituents, their close colleagues, their state delegation, the executive, interest groups, and their own personal predispositions. Just how influential any one of these factors is at the time of a particular vote is extremely difficult to ascertain. Possibly the safest statement is that each vote results from a slightly different mixture of all these factors.

No pretense will be made here of introducing a technique that untangles and weighs these factors relative to the vote on federal aid to education in 1965. Instead, some observations will be made about how the new rationale strengthened the possibilities of passing the school-aid bill. Later, in Chapter IV, data are presented which illustrate that the party variable played an important part in influencing the final vote. However, the party factor is not sufficient to account for the voting pattern on aid to education in 1965. Consequently, the party voting analysis is supplemented by additional empirical data that suggest the rationale and features of the bill helped to secure congressional votes for the legislation.

The first observation has been noted: the rationale for federal aid to education was presented in a novel and apparently refreshing manner. After many years of listening to essentially the same witnesses reiterating essentially the same statistics, showing either the existence of or lack of an education "crisis" revolving around enrollments, classroom shortages, teacher shortages, and state-local tax resources, congressmen certainly must have welcomed the change in presentation if for no other reason than variety. One administration official suggested that the new approach at least did not doom the bill before congressional consideration:

> If we had brought a construction or salary bill to the Hill I doubt if it would have had much of an impact—they [the congressmen] would have said: 'So, what else is new?' As it was, they at least had something new to bat around.[50]

Novelty alone, of course, is not enough to gain political support for a bill. The rationale, whether old or new, which supports a legislative

[50] This and following unattributed quotations are from interviews conducted by the author with various individuals who were involved with the Education Act of 1965. The interviews were held in March, 1966. The questions were open-ended, no notes were taken during the interview, and the quotations are derived from notes made immediately after each interview. The respondents were told that their comments would not be identified.

proposal must be presented in terms that are likely to convince legislators that positive action is necessary. In this sense, the rationale used in 1965 was clearly an improvement over earlier proponent arguments. It effectively focused on educational problems that were undisputedly acute. Whereas opponents of federal aid to education could bring forth reams of statistics, as they did in the past, to "demonstrate" that the classroom and teacher "shortages" were being dealt with adequately by state and local resources, they were unable to cast doubt on the seriousness of the education problems involving poverty-stricken students. The persuasiveness of the poverty approach is indicated by the fact that some congressional opponents of the bill (and of federal aid in general) argued that the legislation was deficient because, among other reasons, it did not concentrate sharply enough on aiding poor students.[51] Whether this argument was made in good faith is difficult to determine. But one fact appears clear: Ideologically, it was difficult for opponents of the bill to be publicly against providing aid that would enable poverty-stricken children to receive an adequate education and, thereby, would allow them to take responsible economic roles in the future instead of becoming public wards.

Not only did the new rationale weaken the posture of the opposition, it also helped to unite the proponents of federal support for education. Aiding disadvantaged students in urban and rural slums was a program that all long-time proponents could back with some enthusiasm. Presentation of the legislation in these terms averted repetition of past instances in which major supporters of federal aid disagreed among themselves about whether aid should be for classroom construction or teachers' salaries or both. From all available evidence, the cohesion among proponents, which is a basic prerequisite for legislative success, was as high as it has ever been in recent years and must be explained, in part, by the context in which the legislation was presented.

The rationale used encouraged the passage of the bill in still other ways. By utilizing the poverty theme, the education bill probably profited from the political momentum of the over-all antipoverty program. As noted earlier, poverty legislation became the first cornerstones laid by the Johnson administration in its attempt to build the Great Society. The Economic Opportunity Act was passed in August, 1964, by a Congress which had fewer liberal Democrats than the Eighty-ninth Congress. Consequently, it is not unreasonable to suggest that legislation

[51] See, for example, the minority report in U.S., Senate, Committee on Labor and Public Welfare, *Elementary and Secondary Education Act of 1965, Report,* 89th Cong., 1st Sess., April, 1965, and *Congressional Record,* March 25, 1965, pp. 5592–97.

presented in 1965 and linked to poverty would be most attractive to the many congressmen who profited by the Johnson landslide in November of 1964 since the President himself was deeply committed to battle poverty and its consequences. Additionally, it is important to note that the poverty formula used to allocate funds to 95 per cent of the nation's counties meant that every congressional district would qualify for some school aid.

Although the point was not stressed during the congressional hearings or debates, it was no secret that the funds made available under Title I of the 1965 Education Act would be allocated disproportionately to aid Negro students since a large percentage are from families with relatively low incomes. Representative Howard Smith (Democrat, Virginia) reminded the House of this when he commented:

> You know, this bill got its steam out of the hysteria that is going on now relative to the minority race. They are the ones they say need education in order to put them on a basis of first-class citizenship.[52]

From the proponent perspective, this fact appears to be another strength of the context in which the bill was presented in 1965. By providing aid to disadvantaged students in general, the legislation also represented an indirect response to the civil rights movement. The bill provided the Congress with a vehicle for at least partially satisfying the needs of Negroes without appearing to "knuckle under" to the demands of civil rights groups.

[52] *Congressional Record,* March 25, 1965, p. 5553.

III. Demand Articulators: Constituents and Organized Groups

CONSTITUENTS AND FEDERAL AID TO EDUCATION

The relationship between a representative and his constituency includes several normative and factual issues in political science. At the normative level, for instance, is the Burkean question concerning the extent to which the representative should serve his constituency's interest but not their will. At the factual level is the empirical problem of determining the actual nature of the relationship between a representative and his constituency.[1] Underpinning both of these perspectives is the basic concept that there is an influential linkage between the represented and their representatives. Relative to this approach, the attitudes of constituents on various public policy issues as perceived by their representative, constitute one, and perhaps the most important, political input influencing his decision-making behavior. Consequently, the behavior of a congressman toward a measure such as federal aid to education may be explained, in part, by his perception of his constituency's attitudes on the question.

According to this framework, changes in policy outputs would result from actual changes or perceived changes in the attitudes of the population, the recognition of these attitude changes by congressmen, and a decision by the representatives to react in harmony with the shift. Unfortunately, use of this framework to explain the change in national education policy is complicated by a number of factors, including the lack of data on a district-by-district basis and the changing membership composition of the national legislature. Such factors preclude an analysis

---

[1] See, for example, Julius Turner, *Party and Constituency: Pressures on Congress* (Baltimore: Johns Hopkins Press, 1951); Lewis A. Froman, *Congressmen and Their Constituencies* (New York: Random House, 1963); Warren E. Miller and Donald E. Stokes, "Constituency Influence in Congress," *American Political Science Review*, LVII (March, 1963), 45–56; Lewis Dexter, "The Representative and His District," in Peabody and Polsby, *New Perspectives on the House of Representatives*, pp. 3–29; and Charles F. Cnudde and Donald J. McCrone, "The Linkage Between Constituency Attitudes and Congressional Voting Behavior: A Causal Model," *American Political Science Review*, LX (March, 1966), 66–72.

42

which would attempt to explain the vote of individual congressmen on the Education Act of 1965 in terms of changing constituency attitudes on federal aid to education. It is possible, however, to explore the nature of nationwide public attitudes on federal school aid and relate this information in a rough manner to congressional action on the issue. Since the unit of analysis in this study is the entire national legislative system, it is reasonable to use national constituency attitudes as inputs into the system and possible sources of innovation.

TABLE 9

NATIONAL PUBLIC OPINION SURVEYS CONCERNING GENERAL
FEDERAL AID TO EDUCATION, 1943–65

Date	Percentage in Favor of Federal Aid	Percentage Opposed to Federal Aid	Percentage with No Opinion
1943	72	18	10
May, 1948	77	13	10
Dec., 1948	62	23	15
1949	66	24	10
1950	66	24	10
1955	68	24	8
Jan., 1957	76	19	5
1959	77	16	7
1961	73	20	7
1964*	40	58	2
1965	49	42	9

* Excludes 258 who indicated no interest in the issue out of a total sample of 1571.
SOURCE: American Institute for Public Opinion, 1948, 1949, 1955, 1961, 1965; Elmo Roper and Associates, 1950; National Opinion Research Center, 1943; Survey Research Center, 1959, 1964.

The approach is structured around several questions: (1) What have been the historical national attitudes toward general federal aid to education? (2) What have been the national attitudes concerning aid to nonpublic schools? (3) Is there evidence to indicate that these attitudes changed between 1961 and 1965? (4) If so, to what extent can the enactment of the Education Act of 1965 be linked to these changes?

Several national public opinion polls, which have been conducted by various survey organizations since the 1940's, provide data concerning attitudes toward federal aid to education. Table 9 summarizes the results available of surveys taken since 1943. It indicates that for the period 1943–61, six to seven out of every ten individuals interviewed expressed approval of federal aid while about two out of every ten specified disapproval. However, the considerable majority favoring federal aid seems to have diminished by 1965, precisely at the time that Congress enacted legislation. This rather surprising development obviously raises some questions about the relationship between public attitudes and congressional policy-making.

At first glance this information would seem to imply that for a long time solid support existed for federal aid; that it was thwarted by the failure of the national legislature to enact a program; and that, when the public support decreased considerably, the legislature acted. There are several considerations, however, which caution against such an interpretation of the data.

First, it is not at all clear that the results of the polls for the period 1943–61 reflect stable, widespread support for federal aid. Information included in two other surveys, one in 1950 and the other in 1956, shows that a surprising number of interviewees were unaware that federal aid to education was a controversial subject. When asked if they had heard or read about the debate in Congress over the issue, on both occasions 42 per cent of those interviewed replied that they had not.[2] This finding suggests that a considerable number of those who favored federal aid did not realize its controversial nature and, consequently, were not likely to have been or to become active politically concerning the issue.

Other evidence also indicates that the general support for federal aid was less extensive than is apparent from Table 9. The proportion of responses in favor of federal aid to education fluctuated considerably when the same question was asked in different polls, and it fluctuated even more when the basic question was rephrased. For example, in May and December of 1948 similar cross sections of the population were asked the same question about federal aid. In May 77 per cent responded affirmatively; seven months later only 62 per cent answered affirmatively, a difference of 15 per cent. Similarly, in a 1947 Gallup poll a national sample was asked the question: "Would you be willing to pay more taxes to the federal government to raise educational levels in the poorer states of this country—or should the poorer states take this responsibility themselves?" Federal aid couched in this context was supported by only 35 per cent of the sample. In contrast, a 1959 sample was asked the question: "If cities and towns around the country need help to build schools, the government in Washington ought to give them the money they need. Do you agree or disagree?" Presented in this form, 77 per cent of those interviewed agreed that federal assistance should be extended. Then in 1964 a comparable national sample was asked: "Some people think the government in Washington should help towns and cities provide

2 See Munger and Fenno, *National Politics and Federal Aid to Education*, p. 92.

education for grade and high school children, others think this should be handled by the states and local communities. Have you been interested enough in this to favor one side over the other? (If yes) Which are you in favor of?"[3] In this survey 16 per cent of the sample indicated no interest in the issue and only 40 per cent of those interested enough to have an opinion favored federal assistance.

Fundamental to all of these questions was the proposition that the federal government should provide some contribution to local education. The fact that such diverse results have been produced by asking the same question at different times and by rephrasing the basic question implies that the underlying attitudes were shallow and certainly were not crystalized enough to produce strong political pressure for action. In this sense, it would be a mistake to place great reliance on the significance of the shifts in opinion since it is likely that the variations reflected the phrasing of the question rather than thoughtful revisions of the public's attitudes. It is interesting to note, however, that on the one occasion when an attempt was made to separate the segments of the public interested enough in the issue to have an opinion only 40 per cent of those interested were in favor of federal aid; this result suggests that the results of other polls overestimated the proportion of the public that was both aware of the issue and in favor of assistance.

In addition to the instability of public attitudes expressed on the issue, there is further evidence to indicate why the apparent broad support for aid did not stimulate the enactment of a law before 1965. Those individuals who favored federal aid for education disagreed among themselves, as did interest groups and legislators, over the kind of aid program desirable. If the questions of aid to segregated schools, aid to nonpublic schools, and aid for buildings versus salaries are introduced into the discussion, it becomes clear that the public support for school aid has been diffused. All three questions were included in a 1961 survey. As shown in Table 10, those respondents favoring aid were split over the terms of the program. The fact that no choice of program had as many as one out of five supporters illustrates the diffusion of public pressure for school aid and in no small way exemplifies why the national legislature did not develop a positive consensus on the issue in the face of what seemed to be widespread public support.[4]

[3] The 1948 question was asked by the American Institute of Public Opinion and the 1964 question by the Survey Research Center.

[4] The case of public attitudes toward federal aid to education appears to be a good example of the point made by V. O. Key, Jr., in *Public Opinion and American Democracy* (New York: Alfred A. Knopf, 1961), that the intensity of opinion rather than its direction is likely to be more crucial in attempting to establish any relationship between public attitudes and governmental action.

Given these additional dimensions of the data presented in Table 9, it is evident that the passage of the Education Act of 1965 was not the result of increased public support for federal aid. In fact, if the 1964 and 1965 polls were at all reflective of public attitudes, less than half of the adult population approved of the action taken.

TABLE 10

PROPORTION OF INDIVIDUALS FAVORING VARIOUS FEDERAL AID PROGRAMS, 1961

Program	Percentage Favoring
All Public—Only Public—Buildings	18.3
All Public—Only Public—Salaries	13.9
All Public—Only Public—Both	12.5
All Public—Also Private—Buildings	12.6
All Public—Also Private—Salaries	8.4
All Public—Also Private—Both	8.6
Not Segregated—Only Public—Buildings	7.1
Not Segregated—Only Public—Salaries	4.8
Not Segregated—Only Public—Both	5.6
Not Segregated—Also Private—Buildings	3.0
Not Segregated—Also Private—Salaries	2.5
Not Segregated—Also Private—Both	2.7
N = 2772	100.0

SOURCE: Frank Munger, "The Politics of Federal Aid to Education," unpublished paper presented at 1965 meeting of the American Political Science Association Annual Conference, Washington, D.C., September, 1965.

PUBLIC ATTITUDES ON PAROCHIAL SCHOOL AID

If the passage of the 1965 bill cannot be linked to greater public endorsement, is it possible that a shift in attitudes on the key sub-issue—aid to parochial schools—occurred and contributed to the enactment of the law? Again national surveys provide a source of information; how-

TABLE 11

NATIONAL PUBLIC OPINION SURVEYS CONCERNING FEDERAL AID
TO PAROCHIAL SCHOOLS, 1938–64

Year	Percentage Opposed to Parochial School Aid	Percentage in Favor of Parochial School Aid	No Opinion
1938	53	35	12
1949	51	41	8
1961	57	36	7
1963	41	51	8
1964	51	40	9

SOURCE: American Institute for Public Opinion, 1938, 1949, 1961, 1963; Survey Research Center, 1964.

ever, the results, as reported in Table 11, although helpful do not reveal some important reservations. On surface it appears that public attitudes on the question of aid to parochial schools displayed little variation for the period 1938–61, during which about 55 per cent of those interviewed opposed such aid while approximately 35 per cent favored it. Additionally, it seems that this two-decade pattern shifted sometime between 1961 and 1963, so that by the latter date a small plurality favored aid to parochial schools; but the earlier distribution was recorded again in 1964.

TABLE 12

PROPORTION OF RESPONDENTS FAVORING FEDERAL AID TO
PAROCHIAL SCHOOLS, BY RELIGION, 1961–64

Year	Total Percentage Favoring Private Aid	Percentage of Catholics Favoring Private Aid	Percentage of Protestants Favoring Private Aid	Percentage of Jews Favoring Private Aid
1961	36	70	31	2
1963	51	76	45	26
1964	40	62	34	27

SOURCE: American Institute for Public Opinion, 1961, 1963; Survey Research Center, 1964.

In order to assess the meaning of thse conflicting changes, it is necessary first to analyze in detail the shift that occurred between 1961 and 1963, since this shift represents an important development in the school-aid fight because aid to nonpublic schools had been one of the major obstacles blocking earlier legislation.[5] During the postwar period Catholic organizations insisted that any general federal aid to education program include equal assistance to parochial schools. Opposition to this demand centered basically among Protestants and Protestant organizations; therefore, an analysis of the shift in terms of religious groupings is essential. If this shift in public attitudes merely reflected a greater proportion of Catholics favoring parochial school assistance, then the political dynamics of the situation did not change significantly. However, if individuals with other religious affiliations also changed their opinions on the question then a new set of circumstances existed.

It should be noted that the shift in attitudes between 1961 and 1963 probably was not due to the phrasing of the inquiry. On both occasions the American Institute for Public Opinion asked a national sample the following question: "If the Federal Government in Washington decides to give money to aid education . . . should this money go only to public

[5] Another portion of this chapter discusses this topic at length.

schools, or should money go to help Catholic and other private schools as well?"

The proportion of the respondents affiliated with the three major religious groups who favored federal aid to parochial schools is shown in Table 12. Not only did the proportion of Catholics favoring nonpublic school aid increase between 1961 and 1963 from 70 to 76 per cent, but a larger proportion of Protestants (from 31 to 45 per cent) and an even greater proportion of Jews (from 2 to 26 per cent) also changed their attitudes.

IMPLICATIONS

Although on a percentage basis the change in attitudes between 1961 and 1963 was greatest among Jews, the total number of individuals changing opinions was greatest among Protestants. Given the nature of past conflicts over school aid and given simple population statistics, this fact, in political terms, becomes the most important aspect of the shift. It is likely that as Catholics and Protestants converged in their attitudes on the issue the possibility of enacting a bill increased. With the segregation issue essentially reconciled by the Civil Rights Act of 1964, and with the construction versus salary question avoided by the terms of the 1965 bill, to what extent can the initial shift in public opinion on the religious issue be related to the passage of the 1965 act? Did congressmen who previously opposed parochial aid view this new development as a mandate to vote for a measure including private school aid?

In order to satisfy these inquiries it is necessary to consider several factors. First, a closer examination of the magnitude of change among non-Catholics provides some revealing clues. The data in Table 12 indicate that, of the Protestants and Jews opposed to nonpublic school aid in 1961, approximately one out of five had modified their opinion by 1963. This rather moderate change, plus the consideration that even after the shift less than one-half of the Protestants and only one-fourth of the Jews favored the proposition, implies that the shift in attitudes on the religious issue was less than a "revolutionary" innovation and was unlikely to have had much of a direct impact on congressional voting behavior. To arrive at an opposite conclusion, one would have to assume that this shift in constituency attitudes was, first, great enough to be brought to the attention of congressmen and, second, significant enough in both size and intensity to convince congressmen previously inclined to oppose a federal aid bill that included parochial school aid to vote in favor of such legislation. The existing evidence concerning the major influences on congressional voting behavior argues against this interpretation. For example, in their study, Miller and Stokes discovered that party policy, the representative's own policy preferences, and his *perception* of preferences held by his constituency were all more influential than the actual views of his constituency on issues other than civil rights.[6]

Further evidence suggests that the shift in attitudes on the religious issue recorded between 1961 and 1963 was unlikely to be a factor in the passage of the Education Act of 1965. The results of the poll conducted by the Survey Research Center in 1964, in contrast to the findings of the American Institute for Public Opinion in 1963, show that a majority of the total sample was opposed to aid for parochial schools and that the proportion of Catholics (62%) and Protestants (34%) favoring nonpublic school aid was considerably smaller than what had been reported in 1963. There is some reason to believe that the 1964 Survey Research Center poll was a more accurate measure of the relevant attitudes.

It will be recalled that the American Institute for Public Opinion phrased its question: If the government decides to give aid should the money go to public schools only or private as well? The shortcoming of this phrasing is that the respondent had to accept the fact of an aid program (whether or not he favored one) and comment on whether some of the money should be given to private schools. In this context, the proportion of the population desiring parochial school aid in a positive sense is somewhat obscured because it is possible that some respondents who actually opposed all federal aid would have been willing to see some aid distributed to private schools if, contrary to their basic position, a school-aid bill were enacted. In other words, this phrasing of the question tended to group together those segments of the population that wanted a federal aid program that would include assistance to private schools and those that were opposed to all aid but felt that if aid must come it should also be given to private schools.

In contrast, the wording of the Survey Research Center's question was more straightforward: "Many grade schools and high schools around the country are run by various churches and religious groups of all faiths—Protestants, Catholics, Jews. Do you think the government should provide help to these schools or not?" With the question posed in this manner, it is likely that only those respondents who favored both the basic concept of federal aid and aid to private schools would give an affirmative answer. For this reason, the 1964 poll by Survey Research Center is probably the most reflective of the state of public attitudes on the question of assistance to parochial schools prior to the 1965 con-

[6] Miller and Stokes, *American Political Science Review*, LVII (March, 1963), 45–56.

gressional consideration of the issue; and it does not indicate strong public support for parochial school aid.

In summary, it is not likely that a change in public opinion on the question of aid to nonpublic schools is an important source of innovation related to the passage of the 1965 Education Act. If a shift in opinion did occur, as the American Institute for Public Opinion's data indicate, the shift was small in magnitude, a majority of Protestants and Jews were still opposed to federal assistance for parochial schools, and there is little evidence to indicate that congressmen who ordinarily voted against a program including parochial school aid felt compelled to vote for it as a result of new constituency pressure.

It would be misleading, however, to neglect completely the possibility that the shift in attitudes recorded by the American Institute for Public Opinion polls may have had an indirect effect on the passage of the legislation. The next section of this chapter, an examination of interest group alignments on the issue of general federal aid and parochial school aid prior to and during 1965, shows that one of the salient developments in 1965 was the modification in position of the major Protestant organizations on the religious issue and the consequent implications of this change for the proponent victory. It is conceivable that the growing proportion of Protestants willing to accept the notion of aid to private schools (according to the American Institute for Public Opinion's findings) meant that the leadership of the major Protestant organizations may have been given a freer hand to make a looser interpretation of the relationship between their previous stance on the issue and their position in 1965. Consequently, the interest groups, given their greater visibility and more direct contact within Congress,[7] may have performed the function of transmitting any shift in attitudes at the grass roots to representatives through their policy statements before the congressional committee hearings on the education bill (H.R. 2362 and S. 370).

THE GROUP THEORY OF POLITICS

The attempt to locate the genesis of political change among demand articulators has led to an investigation of innovation as it relates to changing constituent views as reflected in public opinion surveys. Another and certainly not contradictory way to probe the origin of political innovation involves the group theory approach to the policy-making process.

The group theory of politics was developed lucidly by Arthur Bentley in his book, *The Process of Government*, which first appeared in 1908;

[7] See, for example, Charles L. Clapp, *The Congressman: His Work as He Sees It* (New York: Doubleday and Company, 1963), Chapter 4.

it has been restated and revitalized by David Truman. Truman suggests that in general an interest group is characterized by "a shared attitude" that makes certain claims upon other groups in the society. A political interest group is one "that make claims through or upon the institutions of government."[8] From this perspective most political outputs are basically a function of conflicts among organized interest groups which have resorted to applying political demands upon the governmental system to achieve their objectives. Earl Latham summarizes the concept by writing:

> The legislature referees the group struggle, ratifies the victories of the successful coalitions, and records the terms of the surrenders, compromises, and conquests in the form of statutes. . . . The legislative vote on any issue thus tends to represent the composition of strength, i.e., the balance of power among the contending groups at the moment of voting. What may be called public policy is actually the equilibrium reached in the group struggle at any given moment, and it represents a balance which the contending factions of groups constantly strive to weight in their favor.[9]

Frank Munger has proposed that within the interest group framework major political change may be brought about in two principal ways. First, a major external influence may unsettle the existing equilibrium of groups, thus forcing a new response by both the groups and governmental decision-makers. Second, the balance of groups which produced and supports existing public policy may be altered by: (a) an increase or decrease of the political influence and access of some or all of the groups; (b) a redefinition of group doctrines by the group leaders and members, which in turn generates new combinations and coalitions; or (c) the activation of new participants in the political process with a consequent alteration in public policy outcomes.[10]

The available evidence indicates that, from among these possible means of group-stimulated change, the emergence of a new interest-group coalition supplies the most reasonable interpretation of the group influence on the enactment of the Education Act of 1965. In that year the proponents of federal aid were able to fashion a powerful alliance

[8] David B. Truman, *The Governmental Process* (New York: Alfred Knopf, Inc., 1951), p. 37.
[9] Earl Latham, "The Group Basis of Politics: Notes for a Theory," *American Political Science Review,* XLVI (June, 1952), 390. It is worth noting that some political scientists have cautioned against overstressing the importance of interest groups at the expense of individuals and the legislature. See, for example, Peter H. Odegard, "The Group Basis of Politics: A New Name for an Ancient Myth," *The Western Political Quarterly,* XI (September, 1958), 689–702.
[10] Munger, "The Politics of Federal Aid to Education."

which a weakened opposition was unable to challenge effectively. To demonstrate the dimensions and impact of this coalition, it is necessary to discuss the former group alignments on the issue of federal aid, the nature and basis of the 1965 alliance, and the extent to which the proponent victory can be explained in political interest group terms.

FORMER GROUP ALIGNMENTS

One of the historical characteristics of the movement for federal support of education is the variety of interest group coalitions for and against the various proposals that have been presented to Congress. Throughout the twentieth century several groups have altered their positions on the basic question of federal involvement in education; others have alternated between supporting or opposing federal aid proposals, depending upon the details of specific bills. Among the major groups included in the former category are the Daughters of the American Revolution (D.A.R.), the National Catholic Welfare Conference (N.C.W.C.), the American Legion, and the American Farm Bureau.

The Daughters of the American Revolution voted in 1921 and 1922 to endorse both a U.S. Department of Education and the distribution of federal aid to states for educational purposes. However, late in the 1920's the D.A.R. began to shift its position on federal aid and other issues as its ideological interests gravitated toward fighting the "Communist menace" in America. By the post-World War II period, the D.A.R. strongly opposed both the expansion of the federal government and federal aid to education.[11]

What may be referred to as the Catholic viewpoint on federal aid to education is not always easy to identify because it has shifted over time and has varied from individual to individual and from one Catholic organization to another. However, the organization which represents Catholic bishops, the National Catholic Welfare Conference, and its policies generally have been considered to be the most important index to the Catholic position on the issue of federal aid. From 1919 to 1944 the N.C.W.C. officially opposed federal aid to education on the grounds that the acceptance of federal funds eventually would necessitate the acceptance of federal control over Catholic schools. Presumably, the increased fiscal strain experienced by Catholics in their efforts to maintain a Catholic education system overshadowed the fear of federal control, because the N.C.W.C. altered its view on the issue during the post-

[11] Martha Strayer, *The D.A.R.: An Informal History* (Washington, D.C.: Public Affairs Press, 1958). Also see Munger and Fenno, *National Politics and Federal Aid to Education*, pp. 29–31.

war period. Monsignor Frederick G. Hockwalt, speaking for the N.C.W.C., indicated the revised position in the 1945 congressional hearings when he indirectly endorsed the principle of federal aid, declaring that no federal aid program which excluded some form of assistance for private schools would be acceptable to Catholics.[12] The N.C.W.C. has been joined in this positon by the National Council of Catholic Men, the National Council of Catholic Women, and the Citizens for Educational Freedom, the latter a nonsectarian organization although Catholics constitute a majority of the membership.

Both the American Legion and the American Farm Bureau supported federal aid for education through the 1930's and 1940's. Since the early 1950's, however, both organizations have shifted their views on federal aid to strike a more harmonious alignment with their legislative ally, the U.S. Chamber of Commerce. By 1958 the delegates to the National Convention of the American Legion had voted unanimously to direct their officials

> . . . to present the position of the American Legion to the Congress of the United States and to vigorously oppose any and all legislation before the Congress that seeks to impair, erode or destroy independent and complete state control over public education or which makes appropriations, loans, grants-in-aid, gifts or use of Federal funds or financing either direct or indirect for general public education or school construction . . .[13]

At that time the Farm Bureau had arrived at a similar position which was expressed by its Assistant Legislative Director John Datt before the House Committee on Education and Welfare. Datt stated:

> The Farm Bureau has opposed any temporary program and is vigorously opposed to any permanent program of Federal aid for school construction. . . . In our opinion the instigation of Federal aid to education in the form of assistance for school facilities may actually be a great disservice to our publc school system.[14]

In short, over the years the advocates of federal aid have witnessed the disassociation from their ranks of three major groups and have been

[12] U.S., Senate, Committee on Education and Labor, *Federal Aid for Education,* 79th Cong., 1st Sess., 1945, pp. 302–304. An analysis of the development of this position may be found in Seymour Paul Lochman, *The Church-State Issue as Reflected in Federal Aid to Education Bills, 1937–1950* (unpublished doctoral dissertation, New York University, 1963).

[13] U.S., Senate, Committee on Labor and Public Welfare, *Grants for School Construction and Teachers' Salaries,* 85th Cong., 2nd Sess., 1958, p. 102.

[14] U.S., House, Committee on Education and Labor, *Federal Grants to States for Education,* 85th Cong., 2nd Sess., 1958, p. 432.

joined by the Catholic organizations that favor school aid on conditional grounds.

The presentation of clear-cut group alignments on the issue of aid is complicated further by the fact that the specific features of any bill, particularly as they relate to aid for segregated and nonpublic schools, has resulted in various groupings. For example, the National Association for the Advancement of Colored People has supported general school aid but has opposed any bill which fails to stipulate that funds are barred to segregated schools. Similarly, many religious organizations have supported federal aid but have been opposed to the distribution of funds to private and parochial schools. These organizations include the American Jewish Congress, the Baptist Joint Committee on Public Affairs, the National Association of Evangelicals, the National Lutheran Church, the Protestants and Other Americans United for Separation of Church and State, and the Unitarian Fellowship for Social Justice. In addition, the largest educators' organization, the National Education Association, has resisted aid to nonpublic schools as have a number of other nonreligious groups. The Catholic groups identified above have opposed these groups and have argued against any bill that does not include assistance for private schools.

Although variations exist, it is possible to identify the combination of groups that have been for or against federal aid; but caution must be used in assessing the stability of the coalitions. This taken into consideration, the listings below indicate the major interest groups which generally have taken a consistent stance on the issue during most of the post-World War II period.

The major organizations that have supported federal aid for education are: National Education Association;* AFL-CIO and its affiliates; American Federation of Teachers;* Council of Chief State School Officers;* National Congress of Parent-Teachers; American Association of University Professors; American Association of University Women; Americans for Democratic Action; National Farmers' Union; American Parents Committee; American Veterans Committee; National Association for the Advancement of Colored People (only to nonsegregated schools).

Those that have been opposed include: U.S. Chamber of Commerce; Council of State Chambers of Commerce; National Association of Manufacturers; Southern State Industrial Council; National School Boards Association (opposed since 1961); Investment Bankers Association of America; American Farm Bureau; American Legion; Daughters of the American Revolution.

* Although supporters of federal aid these groups have indicated opposition to aid for nonpublic schools.

The following religious organizations have supported general federal aid but *without* funds for nonpublic schools: American Jewish Congress; Baptist Joint Committee on Public Affairs; National Council of Churches; National Association of Evangelicals; National Lutheran Church; Protestants and Other Americans United for Separation of Church and State; Unitarian Fellowship for Social Justice.

The following groups have supported school aid provided that nonpublic schools also be assisted: National Catholic Welfare Conference; National Council of Catholic Men; National Council of Catholic Women; Citizens for Educational Freedom.

Those organizations that have actively pushed for federal aid have placed their demands in the context discussed in Chapter II. They have stressed such factors as the enrollment explosion, the classroom and teacher shortage, the fiscal strain on state and local governments, the superior tax base of the federal government, and the national stakes in a sound education system.

The groups opposed to federal school aid have taken exception to this reasoning and have argued that the so-called "education crisis" has been vastly overstated. First, they point out that, while school enrollment between 1950–51 and 1960–61 increased by 44.4 per cent, the number of teachers increased by 51.9 per cent; that classroom teachers' salaries increased 70 per cent during the same time period; and that between 1950–60 new classrooms were built at the annual rate of 67,360, or 7,360 more than the needs projected by educational authorities.[15] Second, they have maintained that public education is not a federal responsibility. The sphere of federal services and functions should be limited to those matters that can be handled only by the federal government.[16] Third, they warn that federal aid eventually would lead to federal control of education:

> Federal subsidies mean Federal decisions about school problems which should be left to States or their communities to make. . . . While the present Congress may deny most sincerely any intention of Federal "takeover" in education, subsequent Congresses will find that both more Federal money and more Federal direction are necessary.[17]

And finally, the foes of aid have asserted that in contrast to the fiscal capacity of state-local governments,

[15] These statistics were used by the National Association of Manufacturers (NAM) before the Senate Committee in 1961. See U.S., Senate, Committee on Labor and Public Welfare, *Public School Assistance Act of 1961,* 87th Cong., 1st Sess., 1961, pp. 375–76.

[16] *Ibid.*

[17] Included in testimony of U.S. Chamber of Commerce. See House Committee on Education and Labor, *Federal Aid to Schools,* pp. 282, 285.

the Federal Government is in a precarious financial situation, as evidenced by the balance of payments problem, the impending budget deficit which threatens further the domestic and international integrity of the dollar, the enormous public debt, and the crushing Federal tax rates. These factors point to the conclusion that the Federal Government should be retrenching, rather than extending, its financial commitments.[18]

It is clear that neither set of arguments is more "valid" than the other, but that they represent different perspectives on the same issue. If other decision-making influences are held constant, then it appears from past results that the opponents of school aid presented the more persuasive case to the national legislature. In this sense, the proponent decision to shift the area of discussion to aid for the disadvantaged was well-advised since it introduced an additional perspective on "educational problems" and federal aid which the opposition was less prepared (or less willing) to dispute.

The shift in rationale, however, was not enough in itself to alter significantly the previous group alignments on the issue of aid to non-public schools. An additional modification of past proposals was necessary if the church-state issue was to be overcome in 1965.

In earlier years, the groups on both sides of the religious question had developed involved arguments to support their respective positions. Those organizations in favor of some form of assistance to nonpublic schools argued that private and parochial schools performed the public functions of educating about 7,000,000 students (in 1961) and fulfilling the state requirements of compulsory education; therefore, nonpublic schools deserved an equivalent share of any aid the federal government might provide for public schools.[19]

In addition, those groups supporting aid to private schools pointed to the fact that the "education crisis" involving classroom and teacher shortages which existed in public schools was prevalent also in nonpublic schools. All of the parents who desired to send their children to parochial schools were not able to do so because the schools could not accommodate them. Since both school systems performed necessary functions and were confronted with similar problems, to aid one at the exclusion of the other meant discrimination. To make federal aid available only to public schools would hinder considerably the ability

---

[18] From 1961 testimony of NAM, in Senate Committee on Labor and Public Welfare, *Public School Assistance Act of 1961,* p. 374.

[19] The arguments for aid to nonpublic schools are derived from the testimony of the groups identified in the above list. See particularly the 1961 congressional hearings referred to previously. Also see Neil G. McCluskey (S.J.), *Catholic Viewpoint on Education* (Garden City: Hanover House, 1959).

of the private schools to maintain comparable standards and eventually would result in the termination of the private school system. Such an occurrence would be an injustice to both parents and private school students since it would limit their constitutionally guaranteed freedom of choice concerning education.[20]

Another form of injustice, according to supporters of aid to nonpublic schools, would be performed by excluding private schools from a federal aid program: an additional and undue economic strain on those parents who are taxed to support the public schools, which by reason of conscience, their children do not attend, and who willingly have taxed themselves again to support a nonpublic school system. According to a spokesman representing the Citizens for Educational Freedom:

> Aid to public school children only would place a further double burden on private school parents, and force them to sacrifice more and more just to keep up with a public system buttressed by Federal funds. Congress must consider that there is a breaking point for the private school parents.[21]

Finally, those associations favoring assistance to nonpublic school students argued that such aid did not violate the principle of separation of church and state. They stressed the fact that the Supreme Court had not ruled explicitly against the practice of the federal government aiding individual private school children and cited the GI Bill of Rights and the National Defense Education Act of 1958 as precedents for providing aid to individual students who may attend any school of their choice.

These arguments were challenged vigorously by the groups protesting against the provision of federal funds to private and parochial schools. The challengers believed that such aid definitely violated the principle of separation of church and state as set forth in these opening words of the First Amendment to the Constitution: "Congress shall make no law respecting the establishment of religion or prohibiting the free exercise thereof." They maintained that federal support for nonpublic schools would be inconsistent with the no-establishment clause and, thus, unconstitutional. To buttress this argument they referred to three court cases: *Everson* v. *Board of Education* in 1947, *McCollum* v. *Board*

[20] The reference here is to the case of *Pierce* v. *Society of Sisters,* 1925, in which the Supreme Court ruled that the government may not reserve educational functions to public schools and forbid education by private institutions meeting the standards prescribed by law for public schools. See U.S., Senate, *Constitutionality of Federal Aid to Education in Its Various Aspects,* 87th Cong., 1st Sess., 1961, Document No. 29.

[21] Senate Committee on Labor and Public Welfare, *Public School Assistance Act of 1961,* p. 1254.

of Education in 1948, and *Zorach* v. *Clauson* in 1952; in all three it was ruled that the government may not finance religious schools or religious education. Writing for the majority in the *Everson* case, Justice Hugo Black stated a view which was cited often in this context: "No tax in any amount, large or small, can be levied to support any religious activities or institutions, whatever they may be called, or whatever form they may adopt to back or practice religion."[22]

The opponents of aid to nonpublic schools argued further that the lack of federal assistance did not infringe upon religious or educational liberty nor did it constitute discrimination against private school parents and children. They maintained that

> it is one thing to say that religious liberty forbids the Government from closing down church schools, as the Oregon Legislature sought to do in the *Pierce* case; it is something entirely different to say that religious liberty also requires the Government to finance the schools.[23]

To the Catholic accusation of discrimination, the countercharge was made that it would be discriminatory to tax all citizens to support schools that were not open to all students.

Additional grounds were used to oppose the claims of private and parochial schools for federal funds. The National Council of Churches, for example, affirmed that any substantial aid to nonpublic schools carries with it at least three dangers:

(1) Those seeking to avoid desegregated public schools might attempt to establish segregated private schools with public funds.

(2) Such aid would be used as a precedent for more direct and more substantial forms of aid to parochial schools, thus diverting rather than increasing the already inadequate resources available for public schools.

(3) This type of aid would, therefore, tend to encourage the development and expansion of several competing systems of sectarian schools . . . whose practical results would be the shattering of the American public school system.[24]

RELIGION AND THE 1961 CONFRONTATION

Prior to 1965 the advocates of these conflicting views on aid to nonpublic schools clashed "head-on" during the 1961 effort to enact the Kennedy administration's education bills.[25] As a presidential candidate,

[22] Quoted in Senate, *Constitutionality of Federal Aid to Education in Its Various Aspects*, p. 12.

[23] Statement by a representative of the American Jewish Congress in House Committee on Education and Labor, *Federal Aid to Schools*, p. 970.

[24] *Ibid.*, p. 395.

[25] For an excellent case study of this topic see Price, "Race, Religion and the Rules Committee," in Westin, *The Uses of Power*, pp. 1–71. Also see the *Congressional Quarterly Almanac* (Washington, D.C.: 1961), pp. 210–34.

John F. Kennedy had endorsed federal aid for education on many occasions, both for school construction and teacher salaries. However, he also had stressed that he favored aid for public schools only and was opposed to providing funds to parochial schools. As the second Catholic candidate for the presidency in American history, Kennedy recognized the political necessity of explicitly stating his views on the proper relationship between church and state. He was presented with an important opportunity to respond to critics when he was invited to appear before the Ministerial Association of Houston, Texas, to discuss the religious issue on September 12, 1960. On that occasion he stated:

> I believe in an America where the separation of church and state is absolute—where no Catholic prelate would tell the President (should he be Catholic) how to act, and no Protestant minister would tell his parishioners for whom to vote—where no church or church school is granted any public funds or political preferences.[26]

His statements certainly did not satisfy all the reservations of all Protestants, but they did provide Catholics with additional evidence that John Kennedy as President would be obligated to maintain the status quo on church-state relations.

Following the election, Kennedy established several advisory task forces to study certain substantive areas, including education. The Education Task Force Report was made public on January 6, 1961. Among the recommendations was a proposal to initiate a program of general federal support for elementary and secondary public schools which entailed general aid of $30 per year for each pupil in average daily attendance, an additional $20 per child for states with personal income per student below 70 per cent of the national average, and an added $20 per pupil in the public schools of cities with a population over 300,000. In total the proposed program amounted to about $1.5 billion, none of which would be available to nonpublic school students.

Needless to say the task force recommendations were not viewed with enthusiasm by Catholic leaders. The proposed elementary and secondary program was strongly attacked by Francis Cardinal Spellman of New York City who declared in part:

> I believe and I state that these recommendations are unfair to most parents of the nation's 6,800,000 parochial and private school children. Such legislation would discriminate against a multitude of America's children because their parents choose to exercise their constitutional right to educate them in accordance with their religious beliefs.
>
> I cannot believe that Congress would enact a program of financial assistance and secondary education unless all children were granted equal educational privileges, regardless of the school they attend.

[26] *The New York Times,* September 13, 1960, p. 22.

By denying this measure of equality to church-related school children and their parents, the task force proposals are blatantly discriminating against them, depriving them of freedom of mind and freedom of religion.[27]

The Cardinal's statement may have signaled difficulty for President Kennedy's education legislation, but it did not alter Kennedy's announced position on aid to nonpublic schools. On February 20 the President presented his special message on education to Congress. In it he recommended a three-year program of general federal assistance for public elementary and secondary classroom construction and teachers' salaries, which amounted to about half of that proposed by the task force report. On the crucial question of parochial schools, he stated:

In accordance with the clear prohibition of the Constitution, no elementary or secondary school funds are allocated for constructing church schools or paying church school teachers' salaries, and thus non-public school children are rightfully not counted in determining the funds each State will receive for its public schools.[28]

Reaction to the President's message was predictable; a spokesman for Protestants and Other Americans United for Separation of Church and State approved his stance: "We congratulate the President for declaring that direct Federal aid to church schools at the elementary and secondary levels is unconstitutional." Catholic leaders, of course, viewed the situation differently. On March 1, Archbishop Karl J. Atter, chairman of the Administrative Board of the National Catholic Welfare Conference, indicated the position of the Catholic hierarchy:

1. The question of whether or not there ought to be Federal aid is a judgement to be based on objective economic facts connected with the schools of the country and consequently Catholics are free to take a position in accordance with the facts.

2. In the event that there is Federal aid to education we are deeply convinced that in justice Catholic school children should be given the right to participate.

3. Respecting the form of participation, we hold it to be strictly within the framework of the Constitution that long-term, low-interest

[27] *The New York Times,* January 18, 1961, p. 1. This was not the first time that Cardinal Spellman became involved in a controversy over school aid. During the 1949 congressional consideration of the Barden bill, which excluded any aid for private schools, Cardinal Spellman and Mrs. Eleanor Roosevelt became involved in a well-publicized conflict over the issue. A discussion of this dispute may be found in Lochman, *The Church-State Issue as Reflected in Federal Aid to Education Bills, 1937–1950.*

[28] *The New York Times,* February 21, 1961, p. 1.

loans to private institutions could be part of the Federal aid program. It is proposed, therefore, that an effort be made to have an amendment to this effect attached to the bill.

4. In the event that a Federal aid program is enacted which excludes children in private schools, these children will be victims of discriminatory legislation. There will be no alternative but to oppose such discrimination.[29]

The concluding sentence stated clearly that, if Congress refused to authorize the suggested loans to parochial schools, the bishops would seek to defeat the entire federal aid program.

The adoption of such a posture, to put it mildly, discouraged consensus building, a quality that the movement for federal aid to education clearly lacked. The religious controversy surrounding the 1961 legislation is a good example of why this was so.

The lines of conflict concerning school aid in 1961 were drawn well before the respective House and Senate committees began deliberations on the proposed legislation. In fact, the hearings did little to alter the situation. On the third day of the Senate hearings, March 11, the case against parochial school aid, in the form of low-interest loans or any other manner, was delivered forcefully by spokesmen representing the Baptist Joint Committee on Public Affairs, the American Jewish Congress, and Protestants and Other Americans United for Separation of Church and State. C. Stanley Lowell, associate director of the latter organization, presented the most vigourous opposition by reading from an editorial published by the *Christian Century,* a leading Protestant publication.

> Cardinal Spellman has not changed his mind. His aim is still to compel Protestants, Jews, and others to support a wholly controlled function of the Roman Catholic Church. The compulsion lies in the use of taxing powers of the Federal government to raise funds for Catholic schools. He has given us fair warning, so he should have our answer. American Protestants will never pay taxes to support Catholic schools. We will oppose enactment of laws which require such payments. If Congress is pressured into enacting such laws, we will contest them in the courts. If the courts reverse themselves and declare such laws constitutional, we will still refuse to pay these taxes, paying whatever price is necessary to preserve religious liberty in a pluralistic society.[30]

Two days later Cardinal Spellman, in response to inquiries concerning

[29] *The New York Times,* March 3, 1961, p. 18.
[30] Senate Committee on Labor and Public Welfare, *Public School Assistance Act of 1961,* p. 489. It is interesting to compare the tone of this statement with those made in the same periodical during 1965; for somewhat milder statements see the issues of the *Christian Century* for February 17, 1965; February 24, 1965; and March 24, 1965.

"whether [he] desired to modify or clarify [his] views in light of recent developments," issued an additional statement from his New York office. The Cardinal made it plain that he was "still opposed to any program of Federal aid that would penalize a multitude of America's children" because their parents choose to enroll them in parochial schools. Although he commended President Kennedy for his interest in education and his equitable proposals in the field of higher education, Spellman maintained "the administration's proposal in the field of elementary and secondary schools is not fair and equitable." He concluded:

> Since equitable alternatives are available, the enactment of a program of Federal aid for the children of our Nation that would exclude those attending private and church-related schools would be a great injustice.[31]

The testimony by the representative of the N.C.W.C., Monsignor Hockwalt, was similar in tone. After reviewing the extent of the parochial school system in the nation and its complementary role and similar problems related to the public school system, the Monsignor presented the well-known case for aid to nonpublic schools. He posed the question, "What can be done for the private schools and in particular the parochial school?" Then he provided the following answer:

> We have the courageous example of Government aid to our colleges without discrimination. My petition today points up the need to grant similar assistance to the elementary and secondary schools by way of long-term, low-interest rate loans, with the interest rate computed on an annual basis. To grant Federal assistance to only part of the American educational effort is to deny to the other parts the chance to grow. In fact, it hinders parents in that free choice of education which is essentially theirs.[32]

Senator Wayne Morse, chairman of the Senate Subcommittee on Education, commended Hockwalt on his statement and then made a suggestion that added the possibility, although not great, of working out a compromise on the issue. Morse suggested the creation of a task force composed of senators and representatives of both parties which would attempt to determine the best procedural course to pursue in handling the issue of aid to parochial schools. "They can at least give us the recommendation as to whether or not separate legislation should be submitted in handling this matter."

In response, Monsignor Hockwalt pointed out the obvious reservation from the Catholic perspective:

[31] *The New York Times*, March 14, 1961, p. 21.
[32] Senate Committee on Labor and Public Welfare, *Public School Assistance Act of 1961*, p. 935.

I have a feeling that one measure would pass in this Congress, the Federal aid as such. I have a feeling that a second measure, which would provide for our schools, wouldn't have much of a chance. So I am being very frank with you. Therefore, it seems to us that our welfare should be considered in tandem with the administration bill in some fashion so that that can be done.[33]

This strategy of detaching the parochial school issue from the basic education bill became the key theme of subsequent developments.

Much of the testimony before the House committee was a repetition of that given in the Senate and did little to modify the entrenched stance of the major contenders, thus underscoring the need for fresh ideas if the Kennedy bill were to be given a reasonable chance for passage. It was obvious that the administration's initial attempt to dismiss the question on grounds of constitutionality was ineffective and that some alternate approach was needed.

Two attempts at resolving the situation were made in the following weeks. In the Senate, Joseph S. Clark (Democrat, Pennsylvania) and Wayne Morse (Democrat, Oregon) introduced a "Private School Construction Loan Act" which would authorize forty-year loans, at a low interest rate, for nonpublic schools to construct classroom facilities. In the House, Representative Herbert Zelenko (Democrat, New York) introduced a bill that contained the administration's public school program and a proposal for grants to nonpublic schools for science, mathematics, and modern foreign language classrooms. (Under Title III of the National Defense Education Act of 1958 the government was authorized to lend funds to private schools for the purchase of equipment in these three fields.)

Although reasonable attempts to resolve the conflict, both bills were shelved. Parochial school proponents still were reluctant to endorse a separate bill, and the administration still was against including assistance to both public and parochial schools in the same bill.

The Zelenko bill, although unacceptable, suggested a possible path to compromise. Since many of the programs under the NDEA were due for extension in June, 1962, why not tie the parochial school classroom loans to the extension of NDEA? This approach would provide parochial school supporters with a better chance of achieving their goals than they would have with a separate new bill, and it would not threaten the fortune of the Kennedy legislation.

Apparently, this approach became attractive within influential circles because on April 25 President Kennedy sent a message to Congress

[33] *Ibid.,* p. 937.

formally requesting the extension and expansion of the NDEA. Although the President did not explicitly mention adding loans for non-public schools to construct special classrooms, he did say that it would be appropriate for Congress to consider adding other proposals to his draft legislation.[34] In other words, if Congress wanted to amend the NDEA to include loans for parochial school classrooms, apparently the administration would not object.

By late April, then, the prospects of school-aid legislation began to brighten. During the early weeks of May the respective congressional committees reported the public school bill, and on May 16 the Senate began debates. The bill was passed by the Senate on May 25, 1961, as others had been during the postwar period. The real challenge would be in the House which had passed only one general school-aid bill since 1870.[35]

There is no doubt that the House presents a more hazardous journey for legislation than the Senate. Superimposed over such factors as the relative homogeneity of the constituency of many House members and the short term of office, both of which tend to restrict the capacity for compromise, are the structural characteristics of the House which make it necessary for legislation to pass through two additional stages before enactment. In the Senate a successful bill moves through four stages. The advocates of legislation must secure: first, committee hearings on the bill; second, committee sessions to discuss the bill; third, a positive report by the committee; and fourth, a favorable vote on the floor. However, in the House, once a bill has been granted committee approval it must also obtain a rule from the Committee on Rules which permits consideration of the bill on the House floor and establishes the conditions of debate. If a rule is granted, the bill also is subjected to debate and amendments by the Committee of the Whole. In terms of membership the Committee of the Whole is identical with the House, but in operating procedures there are important differences— the most crucial being that votes on changes proposed for the pending legislation are not officially recorded. Consequently, before a measure is considered on the floor of the House, it may be altered considerably by action of the Committee of the Whole.

After the public school bill was reported favorably by the House Committee on Education and Labor, the next step confronting the

[34] *The New York Times,* April 27, 1961, p. 1. For a discussion of this strategy see Sorensen, *Kennedy,* pp. 359–62.

[35] The House passed a bill in 1960 which differed from the Senate version. However, the House Rules Committee failed to allow a conference, and the bill died. This event is discussed in Chapter V.

bill's supporters was to get Chairman Howard Smith of the Rules Committee to schedule hearings on the granting of a rule. Then they were faced with convincing at least eight of the fifteen members of the Rules Committee to vote for a rule on the bill.

While maneuvering for a rule was being conducted, the Education and Labor subcommittees met jointly on June 1 to begin hearings on amendments to the NDEA, including loans for special classrooms for nonpublic schools. It soon became evident that the administration was not anxious to support aid to parochial schools even in this form.[36] The Commissioner of Education, Dr. Sterling McMurrin, did not take an official stand on the proposals. Secretary of Health, Education, and Welfare Abraham Ribicoff and the President were evasive on the issue. In addition, the chance of the NDEA amendments (if approved by the joint committee) being granted a rule was not good. It could be reasonably assumed that Chairman Smith and William Colmer (Democrat, Mississippi) would join the five Republican members of the Rules Committee to oppose granting a rule. This meant that all of the eight remaining members (all Democrats) would have to support the legislation if the rule were to be granted. However, three were Southern Methodists reportedly under pressure to oppose parochial school aid.[37]

To complicate matters further, at least for the proponents of public school aid, committee members James Delaney (Democrat, New York) and Thomas O'Neill (Democrat, Massachusetts), both Catholics, announced that they would not support a rule for the administration's school bill until the NDEA parochial school provisions also were ready for the House floor. This threat became a reality on June 20 when Delaney and O'Neill joined Smith, Colmer, and the five Republicans to support a motion that no hearings for a rule on the public school bill be held until the parochial school bill was also before the Rules Committee.[38]

One week later the NDEA measure was reported from committee by a vote of 19 to 11. Its future prospects, however, did not appear promising. The minority views included in the report attacked the bill as a transparent effort to provide federal aid for nonpublic schools instead of a measure to improve the quality of NDEA.

Matters culminated on July 18. On that day the public school and

[36] This reluctance was related to Kennedy's thoughts of re-election in 1964. See Price, "Race, Religion and the Rules Committee," in Westin, *The Uses of Power*, pp. 61–64, and Sorensen, *Kennedy*, pp. 361–65.

[37] The three members were Carl Elliot (Democrat, Alabama), Homer Thornberry (Democrat, Texas), and James W. Trimble (Democrat, Arkansas). See *Congressional Quarterly Almanac* (Washington, D.C.: 1961), p. 214.

[38] *Congressional Quarterly Weekly Report*, June 23, 1961, p. 1032.

NDEA bills were awaiting rules, as was the President's aid to higher education bill. A few days earlier Congressman Delaney expressed the view that all three bills should be killed and a new "nondiscriminatory" measure be drafted to permit federal grants to parents of children attending public or nonpublic schools. Therefore, it came as no great surprise when Delaney voted with Smith, Colmer, and the five Republicans of the Rules Committee to table all three education bills. The motion to reconsider the decision was voted down by the same 8-to-7 alignment thus killing education legislation for 1961.[39]

The intensity of conflict surrounding the 1961 school-aid bills certainly did not appear, at that time, to improve the feasibility of enacting future aid-to-education legislation. The battle and its outcome seemed only to solidify the conflicting views of the major religious and nonreligious groups involved. The 1961 action pointed out the absolute necessity of resolving the church-state issue if the proponents of federal aid for education were to realize their objective. For the supporters of school aid in 1965,[40] the devising of an acceptable formula to deal with this issue was a prerequisite for any earnest attempt to pass aid legislation.

THE NEW COALITION

The first indications of the approach the Johnson administration was planning to employ in terms of the church-state issue began to filter to the general public a few days before the President's State of the Union Message, which was delivered on January 4, 1965.

A report in *The New York Times* on January 2 stated that administration sources had revealed that some time in the past the President had sounded out a number of representatives and senators on the religious question. He had found the consensus to be that a bill to provide general aid for teachers' salaries and school construction limited to public schools would be stalled once again by those also advocating aid to private schools. In response to this finding (and, no doubt, to the memory of the 1961 action), the administration reportedly had developed an educational proposal that included assistance to

[39] *Congressional Quarterly Weekly Report,* July 21, 1961, p. 1270. It was possible, of course, to bring the legislation to the floor via one of the three procedures available for circumventing the Rules Committee: the use of a discharge petition, a "suspension of the rules," or the use of "Calendar Wednesday." In fact, the administration in a last attempt presented a limited school construction bill via "Calendar Wednesday." A roll call vote on whether to consider the bill was 242 opposed and only 170 in favor.

[40] The school-aid effort of 1961 created such a high degree of conflict that the proponents of aid did not make another serious effort to push general school-aid legislation until 1965.

private school students by utilizing the "shared-time" concept, the provision of grants for the purchase of instructional material, and the establishment of community supplementary educational centers open to all students.[41]

Although the President alluded publicly to his position on the church-state question in his State of the Union Message by saying "we will aid public schools serving low-income families and assist students in both public and private schools," it was not until he delivered his education message to Congress on January 12 that the means for aiding private school students were outlined explicitly and officially. From the message and the subsequent legislative draft of the Elementary and Secondary Education bill that was presented for congressional consideration, it became apparent that three of the titles included provisions for assisting both public and nonpublic school students.

Under Title I, Financial Assistance to Local Educational Agencies for the Education of Children of Low-Income Families, grants would be allocated to school districts where 3 per cent of the elementary and secondary students, or a minimum of 100 children, were from families with annual incomes of less than $2,000. As indicated earlier, funds made available under this provision were to be used to develop programs to meet the special needs of educationally deprived children. In the process of establishing and executing such programs the local educational agency would be required to take into consideration the number of educationally deprived students attending private schools in the area and make provision for including special educational services and arrangements (such as dual enrollment, educational radio and television, and mobile educational services and equipment) in which such children could participate. The emphasis here was on introducing or increasing, depending on the history of the particular school district, "shared-time" educational experiences in which both public and private school children would be involved.

Title II, School Library Resources, Textbooks, and Other Instructional Material, would authorize a five-year program to make available for the use of school children library resources and other instructional material, including textbooks, to improve educational quality in the schools. Although the materials purchased with federal funds could not be used for sectarian instruction or religious worship, they would be provided "for the use of children and teachers in public and private elementary and secondary schools." The materials to be made available under this provision for use by private school students would be the same

[41] *The New York Times,* January 2, 1965, p. 1.

as those used or approved for use in the public schools of the state. In the event that no state agency was legally authorized to distribute the provided materials to nonpublic schools, the federal commissioner of education would arrange for direct provision of the material and pay the cost out of that state's allotment.

Private and parochial school students also would benefit from the provisions of Title III, Supplementary Educational Centers and Services. This title would establish a five-year program to provide

> vitally needed educational services not available in sufficient quantity or quality, and to stimulate and assist in the development and establishment of exemplary elementary and secondary school educational programs to serve as models for regular school programs.

Under this title a variety of services could be provided, such as counseling; remedial instruction; school health; physical education; recreation; psychological and social work services designed to aid individuals to enter, remain in, or re-enter educational programs; academic services and counseling for continuing adult education; specialized instruction and equipment for students interested in studying academic subjects not taught in the local schools; and modern educational equipment and specially qualified personnel, including artists and musicians, made available on a temporary basis to public and other nonprofit schools, organizations, and institutions.

The planning of such programs would require the participation of state educational agencies, institutions of higher education, nonprofit private schools, and public and nonprofit private agencies such as libraries, museums, musical and artistic organizations, educational radio and television, and other cultural and educational resources. Additionally, the programs would have to provide for participation by students enrolled in nonprofit private schools.[42]

Although the President's program did not furnish direct funds for private and parochial schools (as the construction loans requested by Catholics in 1961 would have), it did offer them participation in developing some of the programs and made it compulsory that nonpublic school students be given an opportunity to share in the educational materials and services provided under the relevant titles of the legislation. The vital question was whether these arrangements were sufficient enough to at least partially satisfy the Catholic demand for equal treatment and at the same time not venture so far beyond the separation of church and state

[42] Senate Committee on Labor and Public Welfare, *Elementary and Secondary Education Act of 1965*, pp. 24–59.

principle that they would produce vigorous opposition on the part of other religious and nonreligious groups.

A partial answer to this question was provided on the day that the President delivered his education message. In a statement on the education message, Monsignor Hockwalt indicated that the proposals had won qualified support from the Catholic hierarchy:

> The major purpose of the President's message is to meet the educational needs of the children. This emphasis on the child, the student, I applaud. Priority is given to children in areas of economic distress. This is as it should be. Improving educational opportunities in areas of proven need will best profit both the children and the Nation. I would urge, however, that consideration be given to other resources available in those areas; namely, the private nonprofit schools. It should be emphasized repeatedly that the beneficiaries of any aid program should be the children wherever their wants are found.
>
> Of great significance is the fact that the President calls for cooperation between the Nation's public and private schools. I have always considered the public and private school systems of this country to be partners, not competitors in education. Our experience in many parts of the country proves the great benefit that such a partnership can be to the children in all schools. The administration's suggestion to extend that partnership poses a new challenge for educators.[43]

This was not a strong endorsement of the President's attempt to resolve the issue, but surely the Catholics could not have displayed too much enthusiasm even if they were more pleased than indicated. A public expression of compromise, not victory, was essential if the possibility of repeating the 1961 conflict were to be minimized.

On the same day of the President's message and Monsignor Hockwalt's statement, the National Education Association (N.E.A.), an opponent of private school aid,[44] issued a statement approving the administration's program as both realistic and "politically feasible" and pledging to seek widespread support throughout the nation. The position of the N.E.A. was expressed by Robert E. McKay, chairman of the N.E.A.'s Legisla-

[43] *The New York Times,* January 13, 1965, p. 21.

[44] N.E.A. policy states that it seeks federal support of public education if such support adheres to, among others, the following principles: that expenditure of the federal funds be only for the purposes for which the states and localities, under their constitutions and statutes, may expend their own public education funds (Title II violates this principle); that the legislation be consistent with the constitutional provision respecting an establishment of religion and with the tradition of separation of church and state. N.E.A. Legislative Commission, *Federal Legislative Policy, 1965–1966* (Washington, D.C.: National Education Association, 1965), p. 7.

tive Commission, who commented: "We're encouraged to believe we're on the threshold of a major breakthrough in Federal support of education in this country." Asked about the church-state issue, McKay said he saw no violation of the traditional separation of church and state in the President's program.[45]

Apparently, the timing and the substance of the simultaneous statements issued by these two influential groups were not coincidental. Individuals involved with the 1965 effort have indicated to this writer that the administration (usually represented by Francis Keppel) conducted a series of individual and joint meetings with representatives of the National Catholic Welfare Council and the National Education Association during the summer and fall of 1964 to discuss "what kind of bill would be acceptable to all the major parties." According to one interviewee, "this marked the first time that the Council began to communicate with the NEA." In view of the statements issued and the consequent enactment of the proposal, communication between the two groups and the administration was effective. Indeed, in reference to these meetings, one spokeman stated that "by the time the bill became public the real battle was already over."

One battle may have been over this early; but if the history of the school-aid movement contains a lesson, it is that anything can happen to an education bill before it reaches its final destiny. Although the administration had successfully drafted a proposal which gained prior approval of both the N.C.W.C. and the NEA, it was still confronted with the task of winning over, or at least neutralizing, some of the other major interest groups.[46]

Some opponents of school aid to nonpublic schools (in any form) warned immediately that all would not run smoothly for the 1965 federal aid bill. Glenn L. Archer, executive director of the Protestants and Other Americans, commented that the program would "erode the United States tradition of separation of church and state. The plan seeks to slink under, around and about the constitutional barrier against public subsidies to church schools."[47] The reaction of other religious and secular groups who were potential opponents, such as the National Council of Churches, the Baptist Joint Committee, the Jewish groups, and the Chamber of Commerce, was unpublicized and probably would

[45] *The New York Times,* January 13, 1965, p. 21.

[46] It is important also to note that the American Federation of Teachers had reversed its position on aid to parochial schools. In November, 1964, the organization declared that it was in favor of federal support for children "in every educational situation," including private schools. *The New York Times,* November 8, 1964, p. 42.

[47] *Ibid.,* January 13, 1965, p. 21.

be expressed at the hearings which were due to begin before the House General Subcommittee on Education on January 22.

On that day, backers of the administration's bill received additional support from an important center of power (at least relative to federal aid for education) within the Congress. Representative James Delaney, the Roman Catholic legislator who was instrumental in blocking President Kennedy's education program in the Rules Committee during 1961, said in an interview that the "discriminatory" approach of the Kennedy proposals for aid limited to public schools had now been avoided by making "the child, not the school, the beneficiary of the program." However, Delaney also warned that should the House Education and Labor Committee report a bill that failed to include any aid for parochial schools, he would "be against it."[48] This announcement made the proponents' task clear: they would have to advance the bill through the committee stage essentially intact and resist amendments that would deplete parochial school assistance and consequently endanger passage of the bill once again at the Rules junction of the legislative trek.

Although the House hearings began on Friday, January 22, it was not until the following Monday that the first major interest group expressed its official views on H.R. 2362 before a congressional committee. Robert McKay, representing the 903,000 members of the N.E.A., reaffirmed the organization's announced support of the bill. McKay described the proposal as "realistic" and stated: "It gives a practicable basis for resolving some of the thorny controversies which have surrounded earlier efforts to provide Federal support of education."[49] The witness enumerated the principles guiding N.E.A. policy on federal aid and said, "The President's proposals do not, in my opinion, violate these principles. In its approach and emphasis the program has the wholehearted support of the National Education Association." Representative Carl Perkins (Democrat, Kentucky), chairman of the subcommittee, asked: "Do you consider the dual enrollment as contemplated in Title I or any other provisions in this bill in violation of the constitutional provision for separation of church and state?" McKay answered, "Mr. Chairman, on behalf of the NEA may I express the firm conviction that this program in no way violates the principle of separation of church and state."

The latter statement was challenged by Representative Charles Goodell (Republican, New York) on the grounds that McKay did not understand the implications of the bill.

[48] *Congressional Quarterly,* February 5, 1965, p. 201.
[49] House Committee on Education and Labor, *Aid to Elementary and Secondary Education,* p. 236.

MR. GOODELL. That is fine. You made the point, but I am not sure you have read the bill. Have you read Title II?

MR. McKAY. I have read the bill from cover to cover.

MR. GOODELL. Do you understand what happens in states that bar aid to private schools under Title II?

MR. McKAY. Perfectly.

MR. GOODELL. The aid will go directly to the private school for textbooks approved by the public school officials.

MR. McKAY. That is not the way I read that provision, Mr. Goodell.

MR. GOODELL. How do you read it?

MR. McKAY. I read it that the instructional material, the library books, the other materials will go to the child.

MR. GOODELL. We had testimony just the other day from the Administration that it is not to the child, but it is to the school or to the library. How do you give a library book to the child?

The issue at point in this exchange was not satisfactorily resolved; Representative Goodell maintained that private schools would be given direct aid, and the N.E.A. official stressed the interpretation that aid would go to the child, not to the school. In fact, this emphasis on providing assistance to the student not the private school became the key theme characterizing the position taken by several other principal groups that previously had opposed school aid to nonpublic schools.[50]

After the N.E.A. stated and defended its position, Thursday, January 28, became the crucial day for the backers of school aid; testimony in the morning was given by the major Protestant organizations and the afternoon hearings included a spokesman for the National Catholic Welfare Conference. Conceivably, this was the day that could "make or break" the school-aid effort in 1965.

Arthur Flemming, former secretary of Health, Education, and Welfare in the Eisenhower administration, was the first witness. Flemming appeared as a representative of the National Council of the Churches of Christ, an organization consisting of thirty-one member communions with a combined membership of over 40,000,000. Reacting to Title I, he said: "We believe that it is a basically sound proposal. We

[50] The reasoning behind this principle may be traced to the case of *Everson* v. *Board of Education*. In this case a New Jersey law authorized school districts to pay transportation costs of children going to and from all nonprofit schools, with the district reimbursing parents of children who use public transit. In a 5-to-4 decision, the Supreme Court ruled that the primary object of the law was public safety, not assistance to private education, and it therefore did not violate the First Amendment. This has come to be known as the "child benefit" principle and was used repeatedly by groups in 1965 to justify their position.

welcome it. We likewise welcome the inclusion of the pending proposal of the concept of 'dual school enrollment' or 'shared time.' " He continued:

> I should underline the fact that our support is for a program under which the Federal Government helps public elementary and secondary schools to make some of their facilities and other resources available to students from private schools. A program for making Federal funds available to the private schools would be opposed vigorously by many of the member communions of the national council. As the general board stated in 1961: We oppose grants from Federal, State or local tax funds for non-public elementary and secondary schools.[51]

In reference to Titles II and III, Flemming expressed approval on the grounds that they were "designed to give assistance to students as contrasted with assistance to private schools." However, he suggested that the legislation be revised to insure that the resources made available under these provisions be administered by public authorities and be retained as public property to be loaned, not granted, to nonpublic schools. The over-all tone of Flemming's testimony was reflected in his concluding remarks. He noted that the church-state issue "has been one of the principal roadblocks standing in the way" of federal aid and a "divisive factor in the life of our Nation." He expressed the hope

> that all concerned, both inside and outside of the Congress, will analyze H.R. 2362 with the end in view of doing everything possible to make it an instrument of reconciliation. I believe that it can be. I believe that President Johnson and his associates should be commended for providing us with this opportunity of approaching an old unsolved problem with a new spirit.

This statement of general approval by the first important Protestant group representative to testify before the House committee clearly added further support for the administration's bill. Other Protestant organizations expressed additional backing for the legislation.

Dr. C. Emanuel Carlson, executive director of the Baptist Joint Committee on Public Affairs, emphasized that the proposal was innovative and would require new thinking about many complex relationships. He noted that, in the past, education and welfare goals often were separated. He suggested, however, that the proposed bill brought these goals into closer context and remarked "we ought not be distressed if we find that these two objectives fused into one involve some

[51] House Committee on Education and Labor, *Aid to Elementary and Secondary Education*, pp. 736–64.

rethinking, some creative work that may take a while to accomplish."[52]
In reference to the concept of dual enrollment, he commented:

> Dual enrollment, to our way of thinking can well be defended as the
> right of all children to programs offered in the public schools, and in
> this instance to programs financed by Federal funds properly distributed
> through public channels to the public school districts and carried out
> in public facilities.[53]

Carlson also suggested that the language of the bill be refined to indicate
clearly where the ownership of materials was to be retained.

The representative of the National Lutheran Council, Dr. Philip A.
Johnson, delivered a statement which was not as positive as the two
preceding statements:

> I believe I would reflect the judgment of the vast majority of our
> people in generally approving the significant new programs which have
> been designed to assist Americans whose educational opportunities
> have been, or are, limited and inadequate.

However, he also cautioned: "It would be ironic if a laudable concern
for improving the quality of education should, by stretching the pupil
benefit theory to the limit, lead to the erosion of the public school
system."[54]

Dr. W. Astor Kirk, representing the Methodist Board of Social
Concerns, indicated that although the legislative body of his church
did not have an opportunity to consider the specific piece of legislation
under review

> the general legislative body in May did express itself with respect to
> increasing and improving opportunities for educating the economically
> and socially deprived. . . . I would say that generally one would expect
> Methodists, or a good many Methodists, across the country, to support
> the objectives of this bill.[55]

The spokesman for the Executive Council of the Episcopal Church,
the Reverend Richard U. Smith, presented the clearest example of a
definite shift in position by an organization on the issue of school aid.
He pointed out that as recently as 1949 the general convention of the
Episcopal church was "unalterably against the use of Federal or State
funds for the support of private, parochial, or sectarian schools." The
1961 convention reaffirmed this position by a resolution which stated:
"*Resolved,* that we stand unalterably against the use of Federal funds

[52] *Ibid.,* p. 771.
[53] *Ibid.,* p. 772.
[54] *Ibid.,* p. 775.
[55] *Ibid.,* p. 777.

for the support of private, parochial, or sectarian schools."[56] However, in response to the "growing inquiry on several crucial issues of church-state relations" a commission was appointed six months after the 1961 convention to undertake a study of the issues. Its report was presented to and adopted by the general convention of the Episcopal church in October, 1964. In part, the commission's report stated:

> The resolution of the 1961 convention, expressing disapproval of Government support of church-related schools, should be amended and supplemented by a recognition of the propriety of the inclusion of such schools in various secular public welfare programs. These programs include the provision of standard textbooks for students in all schools, the provision of equal bus transportation, programs for training of teachers in secular subjects, health and lunch programs, grants for the conduct of research, and provision of scholarships and loans to college students.

The final testimony of the morning was delivered by H. B. Sissel, representative of the United Presbyterian church. His statement illustrated a refined alteration in the policy position of his organization on the question of federal aid to nonpublic schools. He noted that the General Assembly of the Presbyterian Church proclaimed its view on the subject in 1950. At that time it favored federal aid for elementary and secondary public education without subsidizing private and parochial schools. This action was reaffirmed in 1953, 1954, 1955, and 1956. After the legislative "stalemate" of 1961, however, the question was re-examined in 1963 and again in 1964. Although still opposed to the use of public tax funds for direct aid to private or parochial schools, the general assembly stated in 1964 that it

> supports in principle a program of Federal aid to public school systems that would encourage shared-time arrangements to permit students enrolled in private or parochial schools to obtain a portion of their education in public schools.

Assessing the bill before the committee, Sissel commented:

> First, I am glad to see for the first time in many years a very real prospect for the enactment of a significant program of Federal aid to public schools. H.R. 2362 represents a fantastically skillful break in the stalemate occasioned by the church-state dilemma in previous legislative efforts.
>
> Second, the use of the poverty-impacted area concept is a highly commendable device by which to match resources with need. Only the

[56] *Ibid.,* p. 781.

most callous can quibble about the principle of basing the amount of aid on the degree and extent of need.

Third, the encouragement of shared time or dual enrollment arrangements (around which, it seems accurate to say, a growing Protestant consensus of support is forming) provides one of the more creative breakthroughs that permits those who differ on ideological grounds to cooperate on pragmatic accommodation to each other's difference.

Fourth, the complexity, prolixity, and vagueness of this bill in some of its sections is not only distressing, but necessitates the raising of some very serious questions as to how it would be administered if passed in its present form.[57]

The accumulative impact of the testimonies given during the morning session disclosed additional support for the administration's bill among key Protestant organizations and represented a crucial initial success in averting a head-on clash between religious groups over the church-state dispute. The tone and substance of the statements were clearly more moderate and compromising than had been the case during the 1961 hearings. The basic objections to the proposal centered upon who would retain title to the materials made available under Title II and who would control the centers established under Title III of the legislation. The witnesses recommended that in both instances responsibility should reside with public educational agencies.

This atmosphere of "reconciliation" continued into the afternoon session when Monsignor Hockwalt appeared before the subcommittee members. Hockwalt repeated the statement he issued on the day President Johnson delivered his education message and continued by remarking:

> This statement was generally characterized as one of reserved approval and cautious optimism because, in my opinion, the administration's proposals offered a workable compromise in basing its provisions on the child, the welfare of the student . . . Those who work with me share my continuing optimism. We reserve our cautions, however, since the legislative road ahead may be a long and difficult one with the provisions subject to change and amendments.

In an apparent attempt to indicate that the Catholics were also willing to compromise on the issue he pointed out that:

> The formula for participation quite obviously is not based on equality of treatment nor does it pretend that it is. The formula suggested is obviously an accommodation. In our mind this accommoda-

[57] *Ibid.*, pp. 784–89.

tion, as we understand it to be stated in H.R. 2362, presents a challenge which can be met. There are a number of reasons for looking expectantly to the outcome of the Perkins bill.

Diplomatic consensus building on the part of the religious organizations characterized the day's hearings and clearly promoted the chances of a proponent victory. However, the following day, Friday, January 29, the first strong opposition to the bill from a major interest group was heard and outward partisan conflict was introduced into the hearings.

The principal afternoon witness was Dr. Edgar Fuller, executive secretary of the Council of Chief State School Officials, an organization composed of the state commissioners and state superintendents of education from the fifty states and Puerto Rico, American Samoa, Guam, the Canal Zone, and the Virgin Islands. Fuller explained that many of the chief state school officers had not yet responded to a questionnaire forwarded to them by him; therefore, he was testifying on the basis of policies adopted in November, 1964, and on returns from a considerable number of officers. Relative to Title I he stated: "Present indications are that the council and a substantial majority of its individual members will support the enactment." Such was not the case concerning Titles II and III. He asserted that Title II "would use Federal funds, in the face of Federal constitutional uncertainty, to reverse most State constitutions, laws and policies in education. . . . The council's policies clearly oppose the use of tax-raised funds for nonpublic educational institutions whether granted directly or indirectly." In reference to the provisions of Title III he asserted:

> Title III could not be supported under the current policies of the council. The combination of broad Federal administrative discretion in the location, establishment, financing, and scope of operation of such centers and authority to choose among competing projects vest more Federal authority than is appropriate in education.[58]

The basis for these opinions was challenged by Representative John Brademas (Democrat, Indiana) who declared he was "profoundly suspicious of the integrity . . . of these polls." He questioned the validity of Fuller's testimony on the grounds that a nine-page letter preceding the questionnaire sent to the state officers was "highly partisan, highly charged emotionally" and could not produce objective answers. Brademas quoted sections of the letter sent by Fuller as stating:

> The political situation here is not good for the states. President Johnson and the congressional majority have a mandate by the Federal

[58] *Ibid.,* pp. 1118–22.

electorate to overrule many State electorates [Brademas inserted: "I am not sure what the distinction there is."] on segregation, on rural emphasis in State aid systems at the alleged expense of the large cities, and on Goldwater attitudes generally on Federal aid and States rights. They see their Federal attitudes rapidly becoming more common in both State legislatures and in Congress through reapportionment. They are feeling their political oats, and there is much distrust of the States.[59]

Fuller replied that the information contained in the letter represented his own analysis and that the organization encouraged dissenters, to which Brademas rejoined: "Is it not possible you are the dissenter and that the balance of your members may take a different viewpoint?"

After a series of exchanges between Fuller and Brademas, Representative Goodell interrupted by declaring: "The thing that bothers me is that the first time we get criticism there apparently is resentment and an attempt to muzzle the witness." The accusation produced another long series of exchanges and shattered the rather serene atmosphere that had typified the first seven days of hearings.

Criticism of H.R. 2362 mounted during the last two days of testimony. On Monday, February 1, a spokesman for the American Jewish Congress, Howard M. Squadron, reaffirmed that organization's commitment to federal aid for education but stated: "There are three aspects of H.R. 2362 which cause us grave concern. Indeed, we find ourselves opposed to the measure in its present form." This opposition was based on the following reasoning: (1) that the shared-time program would provide a form of financial assistance and subsidy to parochial schools; (2) that there is no difference between the grant of federal funds to sectarian schools to purchase materials and the grant of such materials themselves—both are contrary to the principle of the separation of church and state; and (3) the establishment of centers under Title III must be under control of a public body. "The idea of a partnership between church and state . . . is directly contrary to the entire philosophy of the first amendment."[60]

Leo Pfeffer, professor of constitutional law at Long Island University, testified as an individual with no organizational ties. He indicated that he did not detect any serious constitutional problem in Title I, but that the granting of funds for purchasing educational materials to be used in parochial schools and for special educational centers could not be justified constitutionally on the child-benefit theory basis because funds would be used to support religious schools.

A representative of the American Civil Liberties Union, Lawrence

[59] *Ibid.,* p. 1144.
[60] *Ibid.,* pp. 1531–35.

Speiser, expressed the opinion that the administration's bill as written "could authorize the most dangerous subversion of the constitutional principle of church-state separation since . . . 1786. . . . As now written Titles II and III are clearly unconstitutional."[61] Speiser also suggested that provisions of the bill might encourage the establishment of private segregated schools to avoid the *Brown* decision of 1954. He proposed a number of amendments to the bill. In part, these included a provision against segregation in the dual programs under Title I; a deletion of the section permitting the commissioner of education to provide funds for educational materials for private schools in states where no state agency would be authorized to do so; a provision vesting title to such material in a public agency; and an amendment that no administrative authority over federally financed programs be given to any church or religious agency or institution.

The final major group to testify before the House subcommittee repeated several of the reservations concerning H.R. 2362 that were expressed by the organizations discussed above. Speaking for the National Advisory Council of Protestants and Other Americans United for Separation of Church and State, Stanley Lowell read a statement approved at the 1965 national conference of the organization. In part, the statement said:

> . . . current proposals for Federal aid to education should not violate or circumvent this country's long-time tradition of the separation of church and state. Since these proposals [H.R. 2362] do provide for grants of aid in the form of funds, equipment and personnel for schools wholly owned and operated by churches, we suggest and recommend that such features of otherwise commendable legislation be deleted. We also ask reconsideration of those proposals which would contravene State constitutional provisions regarding church-state relations.[62]

Objections to the education bill centered on Titles II and III. Although a few organizations criticized Title I on the grounds that it would subsidize and encourage the proliferation of private schools, the strongest and most persistent protests dealt with public ownership and control of instructional materials and structures made available under Titles II and III and the by-passing of state constitutions, where necessary, to provide educational material to private school students. In an effort to meet some of these objections, the House subcommittee amended the administration draft bill to ensure, among other things, that a public authority would retain title and administrative control over library

[61] *Ibid.,* p. 1660.
[62] *Ibid.,* p. 1762.

materials and textbooks purchased for students attending nonpublic schools. Such material would be made available on a loan basis only, rather than given, to private school pupils and teachers. An additional amendment stipulated that the supplementary educational centers established to provide enriched educational opportunities for both public and nonpublic school students would remain under control of public agencies.[63]

The subcommittee reported H.R. 2362 with amendments for full committee consideration on February 5 by a vote of 6 to 0. Only the six Democratic members of the group voted for the measure; the three Republican members boycotted the meeting to protest the "hasty and superficial" deliberation given the bill. The full Committee on Education and Labor considered the bill in executive sessions between February 25 and March 2. On the latter date it ordered the bill reported with amendments on a 23-to-8 vote. Two Republicans, Representatives Ogden R. Reid (New York) and Alphonzo Bell (California) voted with the twenty-one Democrats on the committee to favor the report.

The hearings that took place before the Senate Subcommittee on Education between January 22 and February 11 did not reveal any alterations in the alignment of the major interest groups. Consequently, the hearings before both congressional committees indicated that those organizations supporting the administration's legislation included most of the long-time secular proponents of federal aid with the major exception of the Council of Chief State School Officers, which favored Title I but objected to sections of Titles II and III. In addition to these groups (such as N.E.A., American Federation of Teachers, AFL-CIO, Americans for Democratic Action, etc.) the bill gained the general approval of the Catholic groups,[64] most of the principal Protestant organizations, and a number of Jewish groups.[65] The sectarian opposition was led by the American Jewish Congress plus a number of other Jewish organizations and the Protestants and Other Americans. They

---

[63] U.S., House, Committee on Education and Labor, *Elementary and Secondary Education Act of 1965,* 89th Cong., 1st Sess., 1965, H. Report 143.

[64] The nonsectarian Citizens for Educational Freedom split with the Catholics by expressing reservations concerning the bill.

[65] The Jewish community was divided seriously over the bill. Some groups, such as the National Society for Hebrew Day Schools, the Union of Orthodox Rabbis, the American Jewish Committee, the National Council of Young Israel, the Union of Orthodox Jewish Congregations of America, Agudath Israel, and the Rabbinical Alliance of America favored the bill as a measure to support the growing number of all-day Jewish schools. They were opposed by those organizations fearing the breakdown of church-state separation. Among the latter were the American Jewish Congress, the Jewish Labor Committee, the Jewish War Veterans of the U.S., the National Council of Jewish Women, the Union of American Hebrew Congregationists, and the United Synagogues of America.

were joined in their resistance by the American Civil Liberties Union, which also stressed the constitutional "weaknesses" of the bill.

Interestingly, the groups opposed to the legislation on church-state grounds received virtually no support from other nonreligious organizations which traditionally have opposed federal school aid on the basis of fiscal considerations, federal control, and need. Such organizations as the U.S. Chamber of Commerce, the various state chambers of commerce, the National Association of Manufacturers, the American Legion, the D.A.R., and the American Farm Bureau did not take their usual active parts in opposing the school-aid bill. None of these groups testified on the bill in 1965. Consequently, the handful of religious groups, the American Civil Liberties Union, and the Council of Chief State School Officers were the only major organizations overtly opposed to the legislation. Comparing this alignment to the unique line-up of groups on the proponent side, including such strange bedfellows as the N.E.A., N.C.W.C., and the National Council of Churches, it is not unreasonable to suggest that during the 1965 school-aid deliberations the interest group pattern was characterized by the weakest opposition alliance facing the strongest proponent coalition of the postwar period.

Several factors help to explain why the proponent coalition developed the way it did. First, the responsible leaders in the administration (particularly Secretary Celebrezze, a Catholic, and Commissioner Keppel) laid the groundwork. Not only did they consult with important groups separately before drafting the bill to determine what would be acceptable, but they also were successful in setting up discussions between groups, such as the N.E.A. and the N.C.W.C., that in the past had been on opposite sides of the issue and had not even communicated with each other. Further, the administration drafted the bill in such a manner that, while it did not completely avoid conflict over the church-state issue, it did offer enough private school assistance to gain the support of the Catholics and yet not the kind of aid that would have forced the Protestant groups into rigorous opposition. The stress on providing aid to the child and thus expanding the child-benefit theory, the use of dual enrollment programs and shared facilities took advantage of the shift in Protestant thinking that evidently was taking place between 1961 and 1965. The administration was astute enough to recognize the compromising potential of this shift and to incorporate its features into the draft legislation.

Behind these explicit factors concerning the new coalition on the church-state issue lingered the memory of the 1961 conflict. In a sense, the 1961 clash over private school aid actually may have been latently beneficial for the proponents of school aid if one considers the impact of its feedback on the politics surrounding the aid effort in 1965. Apparently, the debacle of 1961 did not result in a termination of the federal aid effort for a long period to come as many close observers suggested; instead, it seems to have stimulated a new determination among several of the key interest groups to reconsider seriously their positions and to search for grounds of compromise rather than run the risk of repeating the 1961 incident. In an interview, a spokesman for one of the religious organizations provided some support for this suggestion:

> No one wanted another eyeball to eyeball episode like '61—a repeat of that would have meant the end of Federal aid for a long time. Since neither side wanted to be responsible for such a development both sides were willing to look for ways to compromise.

Beyond the reminder and feedback of the 1961 religious strife over school aid were several other factors which seem to have encouraged moderate reactions by the religious organizations to the 1965 proposal. Certainly the reform movement in the Catholic church initiated by Pope John XXIII and the Ecumenical Council which began in 1962, and the subsequent ecumenical movement, did much to improve relations between Catholics and other religious groups. Both Catholic and Protestant leaders were not disposed to have the newly developed "ecumenical spirit" threatened by another bitter fight over federal aid to nonpublic schools.[66] In addition, the shift in public opinion among Protestants concerning federal aid to parochial schools suggests that the Protestant leadership could more easily support an "indirect" form of nonpublic school assistance than it had been able to in the past without risking a violent grass-roots reaction.

The fact that the N.E.A. supported a proposal including aid to nonpublic schools requires further comment. Spokesmen for the N.E.A. maintained that they did not compromise their principles in supporting the bill.[67] But surely the provision in Title II that allows the U.S. commissioner of education to supply educational material and textbooks directly to private school students if a state's constitution prohibits such action violated the N.E.A.'s stated principle "that expenditure of the Federal funds be only for the purpose for which the states and localities, under their constitutions and statutes, may expend their own public

[66] The fact that the Pope and the Archbishop of Canterbury met in March, 1966, for the first time in five hundred years was indicative of the new rapport between these religious groups. Another school-aid fight would have threatened this rapport in the United States.

[67] See testimony of McKay in House Committee on Education and Labor, *Aid to Elementary and Secondary Education*, p. 236.

education funds." One can only infer from this contradiction between statement and behavior that the N.E.A. leadership, like the religious organizations, had been reconsidering its position on nonpublic school aid as a result of the 1961 episode. Unlike the religious groups, the public statements of the N.E.A. do not reveal a shift in their principles. However, after so many years of failure, apparently N.E.A. decided that it was necessary to display flexibility and to interpret principles more liberally at a time when the long-sought victory seemed within grasp.

Several explanations have been suggested to account for the lack of opposition by traditional opponents of federal school aid. One spokesman for a fiscally conservative organization stated the opinion that the lack of activity on the part of the U.S. Chamber of Commerce reflected a reaction to the 1964 Democratic landslide. The Chamber apparently felt that opposition would do little to block the bill, given the overwhelmingly liberal Congress; thus it was not willing to become involved in a "hopeless" battle. The Chamber did not want to display, in face of the recent national mandate, an "image" of opposition for opposition's sake. Additionally, it would be better to reserve its political resources for use on an issue when success was more likely.

Other interviewees suggested that while the above opinion may explain the development in part an additional factor was operative. They suggested that the Chamber and other business groups may have been altering their stance on federal aid to education as it became increasingly apparent that the health of the economy is related to the educational level of the population. This is a particularly persuasive argument when aid is put in terms of assisting poverty-stricken youngsters to become employable in the society instead of wards of society.

This combination of a new proponent coalition and a seriously weakened opposition is one of the significant factors contributing to the passage of the Elementary and Secondary Education Act of 1965. The proponent coalition of leading educational groups plus the Catholics and major Protestant organizations meant that more congressmen than in the past could assume that support for the bill existed in their district. With the Jewish groups split over the bill, only those congressmen from conservative Protestant districts would have felt constrained to oppose the measure (assuming an interest group interpretation).

Some commentators have suggested that, given the liberal composition of the Eighty-ninth Congress, President Johnson could have proposed, and the Congress would have enacted, almost any kind of education bill. However, it is argued here that the administration's success in bringing the Catholics into the proponent fold was an essential aspect of the mixture of factors explaining the eventual passage of the legislation.

Strong Catholic opposition probably would have been sufficient, in view of Delaney's statement, to block the bill once again in the Rules Committee. If a bill opposed by the Catholic organizations successfully circumvented the Rules Committee, it would have been confronted by the largest number of Catholic representatives (ninety-four) to sit in the House. This fact must have been considered in the drafting of the education bill even if one assumes, no doubt correctly, that factors other than religion are important in influencing a congressman's vote on school aid. Although it is likely that a majority of Catholic representatives would have voted for a "public school only" bill,[68] it is also possible that a determined minority of Catholic congressmen (perhaps lead by Speaker John W. McCormack) may have formed the nucleus of a coalition that could have delayed, altered, or possibly defeated the 1965 education bill. Consequently, the support of the Catholic hierarchy was crucial for proponent success.

Likewise, a bill that went too far in extending assistance to parochial school students probably would have been opposed by both the Protestant organizations and the N.E.A. Conceivably, such an alignment could have brought the Chamber of Commerce and other long-time foes of school aid into active opposition. It is doubtful that a bill opposed by the latter groups would have passed.

In sum, with the segregation issue essentially neutralized by the Civil Rights Act of 1964, the drafters of the school-aid bill in 1965 were faced with the task of constructing a proposal that would not inflame the church-state issue. Although they were not totally successful, the resulting coalition implies that the bill was indeed, as Sissel had said, a "fantastically skillful break in the stalemate."

---

[68] Even in 1961 77 per cent of Roman Catholic representatives, including Delaney, voted for the motion to consider the school-aid bill that was brought to the House floor via Calendar Wednesday.

IV. Demand Articulators: Political Parties and the President

The discussion so far has dealt with circumstantial conditions, constituents, and interest groups as factors involved in legislative change. Each has been analyzed as a possible source of new legislative input and has been related, directly or indirectly, to the emergence of the new policy output under consideration. Two other principal pressures on legislators and the legislative system, political parties and the chief executive, also must be considered.

THE PARTY ROLE IN POLICY-MAKING

Political parties perform a variety of functions in the American legislative process. To a large extent the parties, among other things, take the responsibility of organizing and providing the leadership of the legislature, establishing the rules for negotiation and decision-making, overseeing the activities of the executive branch, and providing the public, to some degree, with contrasting policy positions on national issues.[1] One aspect of the party role in the legislative process is particularly important for purposes of this investigation, yet difficult to assess. It is the extent to which legislative outputs are a function of party votes. In other words, how influential is party affiliation in explaining the voting behavior of congressional decision-makers?

The obvious difficulty in answering this question concerns the isolation of party influence on the individual from other factors, a process that can be accomplished only by inference. The subjective nature of such analysis is suggested by one political scientist's remark that "the ideal way to

[1] William J. Keefe and Morris S. Ogul, *The American Legislative Process: Congress and the States* (Englewood Cliffs: Prentice-Hall, Inc., 1964), p. 270. The latter point, of course, has been the center of considerable discussion in the field of political science. See, for example: "Toward a More Responsible Two-Party System," supplement to the *American Political Science Review*, XLIV (September, 1950); Austin Ranney, *The Doctrine of Responsible Party Government* (Urbana: University of Illinois Press, 1954); and Stephen K. Bailey, *The Condition of Our National Political Parties* (New York: Fund for the Republic, 1959).

assess the nature and role of party influence would be to get a machine that would look into a person's mind as he was making it up and sort out and measure all the various considerations that went into the final result."[2]

Lacking such a machine, political scientists have resorted to roll call analysis, which enables an investigator to determine the degree to which members of the same political party vote together on issues and the composition of deviating voting blocks. In an analysis of the proportion of party members voting in harmony during the various congressional sessions between 1921 and 1948, Julius Turner found that "party pressure seems to be more effective than any other pressure on congressional voting, and is discernible on nearly nine-tenths of the roll calls examined."[3] The significance of party voting also has been pointed out by Lewis Froman, who shows that for the years 1957 through 1961 the proportion of roll call votes in both the Senate and House that had a majority of Democrats opposing a majority of Republicans was 42, 50, 42, 47, and 58 per cent, respectively.[4] In sum, the party model of policy-making asserts that the most prominent factor affecting a legislator's voting behavior is his party affiliation.

Within this framework, legislative innovation may be brought about in two principal ways: (1) one or both of the major parties may assume a new policy posture on an issue; (2) the party ratios may be altered as a result of an election that produces a new party majority. The available evidence indicates that the latter possibility is applicable in this case. Consequently, the question is to what extent can the passage of the Education Act of 1965 be related to the overwhelming Democratic landslide of 1964? Did the Democratic gain of 2 senators and 38 representatives, giving the Democrats a plurality of 36 in the Senate and 155 in the House, help or hinder the chances of federal school aid in 1965?

THE PARTIES AND FEDERAL AID TO EDUCATION

In order to answer the above questions it is necessary to compare the publicly announced stance (via national party platforms) of the Democratic and Republican parties on federal aid, the overt voting behavior of Democrats and Republicans on key roll call votes involving enlarged

---

[2] Neil A. McDonald, *The Study of Political Parties* (New York: Doubleday and Company, 1955), p. 70.

[3] Turner, *Party and Constituency: Pressures on Congress,* p. 23.

[4] Froman, *Congressmen and Their Constituents,* p. 88. Also see Duncan MacRae, Jr., *Dimensions of Congressional Voting* (Berkeley: University of California Press, 1958) and David B. Truman, *The Congressional Party* (New York: John Wiley and Sons, 1959).

federal responsibilities in domestic affairs, and the preferences of Democrats and Republicans on past federal aid to education roll call votes.

A review of party platforms in the postwar era reveals that the Democratic party consistently has favored federal aid for education and the Republican party generally has opposed such legislation, although the Republicans supported limited aid in 1956 and 1960.

The Republicans included no mention of the school-aid issue in their 1944 platform, but the Democrats made their position clear by stating: "We favor Federal aid to education administered by the states without interference by the Federal Government."[5] Four years later the Republicans once more avoided the issue by merely saying: "We favor equality of educational opportunity for all and the promotion of education and educational facilities."[6] The Democrats expressed a much stronger stance on the issue and accented the partisan nature of the question.

> We advocate Federal aid for education administered by and under the control of the state. We vigorously support the authorization, which was so shockingly ignored by the Republican 80th Congress, for the appropriation of $300 million as a beginning of Federal aid to the states to assist them in meeting the present educational needs. We insist upon the right of every American child to obtain a good education.[7]

By 1952 the two parties had taken clearly opposing positions on the issue of federal assistance for education. The Democratic platform pledged "immediate consideration for those school systems which need further legislation to provide Federal aid for new school construction, teachers' salaries and school maintenance and repairs." In contrast, the Republican platform stated: "The tradition of public education, tax-supported and free to all, is strong with our people. The responsibility for sustaining this system of popular education has always rested upon the local community and the States. We subscribe fully to this principle."[8]

In 1956 the Republicans indicated a moderate alteration in their position. The Eisenhower administration had proposed a limited school construction program, and the platform pledged that the party would "renew its efforts to enact a program based on sound principles of need and designed to encourage increased state and local efforts to build more

---

[5] Kirk H. Porter and Donald B. Johnson, *National Party Platforms, 1840–1960* (Urbana: University of Illinois Press, 1961), p. 403.

[6] *Ibid.,* p. 453.

[7] *Ibid.,* p. 433.

[8] *Ibid.,* p. 504.

classrooms." The Democrats re-emphasized their commitment to federal aid by recommending a broad program:

> The resources of our States and localities are already strained to the limit. Federal aid and action should be provided . . . to assist States and local communities to build schools, and to provide essential health and safety services for all school children; for better educational, health and welfare opportunities for children of migratory workers; for training teachers of exceptional children; and for the training of teachers to meet the critical shortage in technical and scientific fields.[9]

During the 1960 campaign the two parties again expressed conflicting views on the issue. The Republicans endorsed limited federal involvement in financing classroom construction only. Their platform stated:

> The Federal government should assist selectively in strengthening education. . . . We believe moreover that any large plan of Federal aid to education, such as direct contributions to or grants for teachers salaries can only lead ultimately to Federal domination and control of our schools.[10]

Senator John F. Kennedy, the Democratic presidential candidate in 1960, endeavored to make federal school aid a major election issue. He criticized the limited support given by President Eisenhower and attacked Republican candidate Vice-President Richard Nixon for backing a limited construction program and referring to federal aid for education as "too extreme."[11] The Democratic platform reviewed the nature of the educational "crisis" existing in America and stated:

> Only the Federal Government is not doing its part. For eight years, measures for the relief of the education crisis have been held up by the cynical maneuvers of the Republican Party in Congress and the White House. We believe that America can meet its educational obligations only with generous Federal financial support.[12]

The 1964 presidential campaign was characterized by the vast differences in the ideological positions of the candidates and the parties. The Republican convention[13] was captured and controlled by the more conservative elements of the party whose leader, Senator Barry Goldwater, promised to provide American voters with a real choice, not an echo, to select between two perspectives of American life. Among the many election issues, the Goldwater crusade against centralized government is

[9] *Ibid.,* p. 535.
[10] *Ibid.,* p. 615.
[11] Sorensen, *Kennedy,* p. 200.
[12] Porter and Johnson, *National Party Platforms,* p. 590.
[13] See White, *The Making of the President, 1964,* Chapter 7.

most relevant to federal aid for education. Goldwater was a long-time critic of the expanding role of the federal government; over the years he had denounced farm subsidies, advocated the abolition of Rural Electrification, and urged the selling of the Tennessee Valley Authority. Speaking before the Senate Subcommittee on Education in 1961, he expressed his views on federal aid for education:

> It is my strong belief that most of these proposals [education bills], including the bill, S. 1021, sponsored by the adminstration, are both unnecessary and unsound. I am convinced that they represent another long step in the direction of reducing our State and local governments to mere subordinate, administrative divisions of the central government in Washington.
>
> I wish to make it clear that I do not believe that we have an educational problem which requires any form of Federal grant-in-aid program to the States.[14]

In contrast to Goldwater, President Johnson, as the Democratic party standard-bearer, was a strong advocate of the strengthened role of the federal government and the strongest supporter of federal aid for education to occupy the White House. His platform pledged further and more comprehensive federal aid to supplement those programs enacted by the "Education Congress of 1963."[15]

This brief review of party statements illustrates that at least at the verbal level the Democratic party has been a more enthusiastic champion of federal school aid than the Republican party has been. While Republicans have endorsed limited aid on occasion, the Democrats consistently have called for an expanded federal financial commitment to education. Further, during the 1964 campaign, the ideological gap between the parties on this issue, and others, was probably the greatest it had been in years. This gap and the subsequent election outcome would suggest that the impressive Democratic victory in 1964 undoubtedly increased the possibilities of enacting a federal aid for education program. However, it is common knowledge that party platforms are, at best, a rough index to actual political behavior; therefore, an assessment of the party dimension in this study requires an examination of concrete action if credence is to be granted to the platform statements.

Party policy differences may be identified in a more empirical manner through the analysis of particular roll call votes. *Congressional Quarterly,* for example, has utilized key roll call votes on such issues as area redevelopment, temporary unemployment compensation, aid for education,

[14] U.S., Senate, Committee on Labor and Public Welfare, *Public School Assistance Act of 1961,* 87th Cong., 1st Sess., 1961, pp. 538–39.

[15] Porter and Johnson, *National Party Platforms,* Supplement, 1964, p. 4.

housing, public power, manpower retraining, stand-by public works, and Social Security medicare to indicate the extent to which Democrats and Republicans vote for legislation that would tend to enlarge the federal government's domestic responsibilities. Since aid for education is a component of this broader issue, it is worthwhile to note the differences that have been found.

TABLE 13
PERCENTAGE OF DEMOCRATS AND REPUBLICANS VOTING TO
ENLARGE FEDERAL ROLE, 1959–64

	Both Chambers	Senate	House
86th Congress (1959–60)			
Democrats	74	74	74
Republicans	19	27	17
87th Congress (1961–62)			
Democrats	75	65	78
Republicans	24	26	24
88th Congress (1963–64)			
Democrats	75	79	74
Republicans	40	47	40
Mean			
Democrats	75	73	75
Republicans	28	33	27

SOURCE: *Congressional Quarterly Almanac,* 1960, 1962, and 1964.

Table 13 shows that during three recent Congresses about 75 per cent of the Democrats voted for such legislation whereas a little less than 30 per cent of the Republicans did so. This finding, in conjunction with the party statements included above, adds support to the proposition that the enlarged Democratic majority in the Eighty-ninth Congress, resulting from the 1964 election, enhanced the possibility of enacting federal school-aid legislation.

Further support for the proposition may be derived from another set of statistics. An examination of roll call votes, by party, on federal aid bills that reached the floors of the two congressional chambers after World War II reveals several factors. First, as shown by Table 14, in both the Senate and the House a majority of Democrats have voted for school-aid legislation while, with the exception of Republican senators in 1948 and 1949, a majority of Republicans have voted against the same proposals. It is also apparent from the table that the proportion of Democratic senators approving school-aid bills has been consistently higher than their counterparts in the House—an average of 85 per cent of the senators compared to 64 per cent of the representatives. This fact, in part, explains why prior to 1965 the Senate passed school-aid bills on four occasions in the postwar period in contrast to the single instance (1960) a bill was approved in the House. Another point is supported by the data in Table 14. A comparison of the relative proportions of party members voting for federal aid indicates that the issue has become increasingly partisan. An uncomplicated index of partisanship, the difference between the percentages of Democrats and Republicans voting for

TABLE 14
PERCENTAGE OF DEMOCRATS AND REPUBLICANS VOTING
FOR FEDERAL AID, 1948–65

Year	Senate			House		
	Dem.	Rep.	Index	Dem.	Rep.	Index
1948	86.1	61.4	24.7	—	—	—
1949	92.3	64.7	27.6	—	—	—
1956	—	—	—	53.1	38.7	14.4
1957	—	—	—	56.5	41.0	15.5
1960	77.8	29.0	48.8	62.5	32.4	30.1
1961	77.4	26.7	50.7	66.7	3.6	63.1
1965	93.3	56.3	37.0	80.0	26.7	53.3
Mean	85.3	47.6	37.7	63.7	28.5	35.3

SOURCE: For years 1948–61, Munger and Fenno, *National Politics and Federal Aid to Education.* For 1965, *Congressional Quarterly Weekly Report,* April 2, 1965, pp. 600–601, and April 16, 1965, p. 691.

federal aid on these roll call votes, shows that the variance between Democratic and Republican support for federal aid has increased over the years, particularly in the House where Democratic approval has steadily grown and Republican support has decreased.

THE PARTIES AND THE 1965 EDUCATION ACT

The vote on the 1965 Education Act was clearly in line with the partisan trends. The measure was supported in both the Senate and the House by a larger proportion of Democrats than on any earlier voting occasion. Additionally, in the House 80 per cent of the Democrats voted for the bill while only 27 per cent of the Republicans supported it. In the Senate the difference was smaller, but the overwhelming proportion (93 per cent) of Democrats cast their votes for the proposal while slightly more than half (56 per cent) of the Republican senators did the same.

Given the Democratic party's commitment to school aid, and given the voting behavior of Democrats and Republicans on the 1965 bill, it becomes apparent that the Democratic victory in the 1964 congressional elections, particularly in the House where the Democrats experienced a net gain of thirty-eight seats, was one of the key factors in the eventual passage of the 1965 Education Act. Indeed, every one of the forty-eight newly elected Democrats in the House who filled a seat formerly held by a Republican voted for the Elementary and Secondary Education Act of 1965.[16] An equally interesting statistic appears in Table 15 which shows that, of the 201 non-Southern Democrats voting on the bill, 197 supported it while a mere 4 opposed. This margin meant that the proponents needed only twenty-one votes gathered from Southern Democrats and/or Republicans to enact the measure in the House, where majorities for federal aid had been most difficult to realize.

The above evidence all points to the conclusion that the Democratic victory in 1964 presented the administration with an unusual opportunity to enact a federal school-aid program. The gain of two Democratic senators reaffirmed the already existing liberal majority in the Senate, while the increase in the House resulted in the largest number of Democratic representatives (295) and the greatest Democratic plurality (155) since the days of the New Deal. With this numerical advantage, the administration forces were faced with drafting a bill that would not split the Democratic majority over such perennial issues as segregation, religion, and the allocation of funds.

As Table 15 shows, three-fourths of the Democratic senators from southern states voted for the bill, whereas in the House a majority of the southern representatives opposed the measure. The southern response in the Senate versus the House may be explained in part by the more heterogeneous constituency of even southern senators in contrast to the relative homogeneous constituency of representatives. Beyond this point, the southern vote in the House implies that for many southern representatives the Civil Rights Act of 1964 by no means settled the issue concerning federal aid and segregated schools. Although the *Brown* decision outlawed segregated schools and the recent civil rights legislation barred federal funds to such schools, the South successfully resisted large-scale desegregation of its educational facilities. In fact, only 2 per cent of the Negro students in the South were attending integrated schools in 1964.[17] Consequently, it is understandable that many southern representatives perceived the Education Act of 1965 as another central government weapon which would be used to undermine the traditional southern school system. It is not unreasonable to suggest that this kind of relationship between federal aid and federal control was disturbing Representative Howard Smith as he spoke on the House floor against the bill:

[16] Computed from *Congressional Quarterly Weekly Report,* January 16, 1965, pp. 16–17, and April 2, 1965, pp. 600–601.
[17] *Southern Educational Reporting Service,* December, 1964.

Mr. Speaker, we apparently have come to the end of the road so far as local control over our education in public facilities is concerned. I abhor that. There is nothing dearer to the American home than the neighborhood school, where you have your PTA and your different organizations, and all take a vital interest in the school and have some control of it. I hate to see that tradition destroyed and that control removed from the little neighborhood in the county and located in the bureaucracy of Washington, but I think I see the handwriting on the wall. This is the great day that the bureaucrats in the Education Department have looked forward to and have fought for a good many years.[18]

TABLE 15
PARTY VOTE ON EDUCATION ACT OF 1965

	Senate		House	
	Yea	Nay	Yea	Nay
Non-Southern Democrats	40	0	197	4
Southern Democrats	15	4	31	53
Total Democrats	(55)	(4)	(228)	(57)
Republicans	18	14	35	96
Total	73	18	263	153

SOURCE: Computed from *Congressional Quarterly Weekly Report*, April 2, 1965, pp. 600–601, and April 16, 1965, p. 691.

In spite of the lingering of the racial question in the minds of some, the bill did receive enough southern support so that the Democratic vote alone (228 to 57) was sufficient to gain passage of the bill in the House and in the Senate as well (55 to 4).

Another issue that contained the potential for splitting the large Democratic majority was, of course, the religious question discussed in Chapter III. As was pointed out earlier, Roman Catholics constituted the largest denominational group in the Eighty-ninth Congress (107). Had an episode similar to the 1961 religious conflict been repeated and had Catholic schools been excluded from the legislation, it is possible that the Democratic Roman Catholics would have defeated the proposal in the House. Such an occurrence was unlikely, for there is little evidence that Catholic representatives would have voted as a block against a federal aid bill that excluded assistance to parochial schools. Indeed, even the "watered-down" public school bill brought to the House floor in 1961 via Calendar Wednesday was supported by 77 per cent of the Catholics in the House (see Table 16). This support suggests that Catholic opposition to a particular aid bill generally would not be problematic for the proponents as a result of Catholics voting en masse

[18] *Congressional Record*, March 24, 1965, p. 5553.

on the floor. It is more likely that Catholic organizations could threaten a bill they opposed by exerting pressure at the committee level, particularly in the Rules Committee as was the case in 1961, or by encouraging sympathetic representatives to establish a coalition with House members opposed to school aid on other grounds. That Democratic Roman Catholic congressmen were satisfied with the 1965 bill is evident from Delaney's vote in the Rules Committee and from the fact that only three of them opposed the bill while eighty-nine cast their vote for it.

TABLE 16

VOTE OF ROMAN CATHOLIC CONGRESSMEN ON SCHOOL-AID ROLL CALL, 1961 AND 1965

	1961			1965		
	Yea	Nay	Per-cent-age Yea	Yea	Nay	Per-cent-age Yea
House						
Democratic Catholics	65	7	90	78	2	98
Republican Catholics	2	13	13	6	7	46
Total	67	20	77	84	9	90
Senate						
Democratic Catholics	6	3	66	11	1	92
Republican Catholics	0	1	0	1	1	50
Total	6	4	60	12	2	86

SOURCE: Compiled from *Congressional Quarterly Almanac*, 1961 and 1965.

Finally, one other issue held a latent possibility for dividing the Democratic block. Republican opponents of the administration's bill presented the argument that the formula for Title I resulted in an "absurd distribution of funds" since the most affluent school districts in the nation, which could well afford special educational services for their disadvantaged students, would obtain federal assistance. Republicans pointed out that the ten wealthiest counties in the nation, containing about 32,000 eligible children, would receive a total of $8,918,087 compared with $4,507,149 which would be granted to a sample of ten poor counties with a similar number of children.[19] Supporters of the administration's formula countered by asserting that the federal contribution to the ten wealthy counties would amount to only 1.9 per cent of their 1962 educational expenditures, whereas the funds allocated to the ten poor counties would be equivalent to 34.2 per cent of their 1962 expenditures. Proponents also argued that it was more costly to

[19] See the Minority Views in House Committee on Education and Labor, *Elementary and Secondary Education Act of 1965*, pp. 70–71.

educate a student in the North, particularly in urban slums, than it was in the South.[20]

Congresswoman Edith Green (Democrat, Oregon), a strong supporter of federal aid, found the counterargument unconvincing. Noting that since the formula was tied to one-half the state's per pupil expenditures it resulted in a distribution pattern which would give Mississippi $120 and New York $353 per "poor" child, she inquired: ". . . where is the justice, where is the equity in this, to give the State which has the highest or one of the highest per capita incomes the most money?"[21] She offered an amendment that would grant a straight $200 for each child from a low-income family; in support of her proposal she stated:

> Mr. Chairman, I really am serious in saying to my liberal colleagues, those of you who honestly and sincerely have been terribly concerned about the events in Selma, concerned about events in Mississippi during the last 2 or 3 years: Are you really shedding crocodile tears? Are we making pious statements about how awful things are and how we really want to do something about it, and then, when we have a bill that is before the House, we do the very least for these States of any single in the Nation?[22]

Representative Claude Pepper (Democrat, Florida) respectively suggested that Mrs. Green had misunderstood the allocation principle underpinning the bill. He stated:

> This bill is not designed to bring the expenditure for all children in the elementary and secondary schools of America up to the same level. . . . It is to help the local community bring the educational expenditure for deprived children up to the level of the ordinary children. . . . That is what the gentlewoman overlooks.[23]

Congressman James G. O'Hara (Democrat, Michigan) warned against the "divide and conquer" possibility implicit in tampering with the formula:

> Many of those who are supporting this amendment and who intend to vote for this amendment are doing so not with the intention of supporting this bill if the amendment passes, but with the intention of opposing this bill regardless and they hope that others will join them if the change they advocate is agreed to. . . . If we want this bill we had better protect this formula.[24]

[20] *Congressional Record*, March 24, 1965, pp. 5560–62.
[21] *Ibid.*, p. 5778.
[22] *Ibid.*, p. 5779.
[23] *Ibid.*, p. 5811.
[24] *Ibid.*, p. 5813.

The Green amendment was defeated, by a vote of 136 to 202, as were several other attempts to revise or delete the formula. In fact, the administration forces retained enough cohesion to defeat nineteen proposed amendments, so the bill was passed essentially in the form reported by the House Education and Labor Committee.[25] Consequently, the large Democratic majority was not seriously split by any of the controversial issues that traditionally had complicated the proponent effort.

TABLE 17
VOTE OF REPUBLICAN HOUSE MEMBERS FOR
SCHOOL AID, BY REGION, 1965

Region	Number of Republican Districts	Number Voting Yes on School Aid	Percentage of Total 35 Yes Votes Cast by this Region
Northeast	38	22	63
Border	7	4	11
Midwest	54	5	14
South	16	0	0
West	25	4	11
Total	140	35	99*

* Does not total 100 per cent due to rounding.
SOURCE: Compiled from *Congressional Quarterly Weekly Report,* April 2, 1965, pp. 600–601.

Thus far the stress has been on the extent to which the shift in party ratios resulting from the 1964 election, particularly in the House, was instrumental in promoting the passage of the 1965 Education Act. However, as Table 1 shows, the final House vote on school aid in 1965 was not only due to increased support among Democrats in the North (where most of the formerly held Republican districts were captured by the Democrats in 1964) but among Southern Democrats and Republicans as well. Consequently, variables other than party must be considered in analyzing the 1965 aid vote of Republicans and Southern Democrats. It is in this respect that the new rationale used by proponents of the proposal plays a role in understanding the 1965 voting pattern on federal school aid. The data suggest that the emphasis on aiding poverty-stricken students in urban centers not only gained the overwhelming support of Northern Democrats, but presumably was responsible, in part, for the fact that a considerable number of Republicans and Southern Democrats representing highly urban districts voted for the bill.

[25] The only floor amendment accepted was proposed by Robert Griffin (Republican, Michigan) and authorized the commissioner of education to appoint a ten-member advisory council to consult with concerning his functions under the act.

Concerning the Republican vote, the impact of the new rationale may be illustrated in two ways. An analysis of the number of House Republicans voting for the proposal by region of the country indicates that, of the total 35 yes votes cast by Republicans, 22 votes, or 63 per cent, were registered by Republicans from the most urbanized section of the country, the Northeast (see Table 17). Indeed, 43 per cent (15 votes) of the total Republican yes votes were recorded by representatives from New York (8) and Pennsylvania (7), both highly urbanized states. This relationship between Republican yes votes and

TABLE 18
PROPORTION OF REPUBLICANS VOTING FOR SCHOOL AID,
BY PERCENTAGE OF DISTRICT URBAN, 1965

Percentage of District Urban	Total Districts	Number Voting Yes on School Aid	Percentage Voting Yes
High Urban (70–100%)	53	22	42
Medium Urban (40–69%)	68	9	13
Low Urban (0–39%)	19	4	21
Total	140	35	25

SOURCE: Compiled from U.S. Bureau of the Census, *Congressional District Data Book* (Washington: U.S. Government Printing Office, 1963) and *Congressional Quarterly Weekly Report*, April 2, 1965, pp. 600–601.

urbanism is denoted more specifically by Table 18. This table shows that when Republican districts are grouped according to the proportion of the population which is urban, the representatives from the highly urban districts (70–100%) contributed almost two-thirds of all the Republican votes for federal school aid in 1965. Among the representatives from these highly urban districts, 42 per cent voted for the aid legislation while only 13 per cent and 21 per cent of the representatives in the less urban categories favored the proposal. In sum, the bulk of the Republican support for the Education Act of 1965 came primarily from congressmen representing urban districts, particularly those in the eastern portion of the nation. Certainly the substance of the 1965 act must have facilitated the decision made by these Republicans to cross party lines on the issue.

As was noted earlier, the majority of Southern Democrats voted against the Education Act of 1965 (53 to 31), as they did against the aid bills of 1960 (87 to 0) and 1961 (70 to 21). Consequently, the Southern Democrats in the House who supported the 1965 bill constituted a deviant group among their southern colleagues. Although it is not possible to isolate the factors which account for the behavior of each of these 31 southern representatives, it is possible to note some group characteristics. For example, at least 25 of the 31 may be considered, in terms of their roll call votes in 1965, as "liberals" relative to other Southern Democrats in the House. This conclusion is based on the data included in Table 19 which shows the frequency in which

TABLE 19

SOUTHERN DEMOCRATIC VOTES ON THIRTEEN ROLL CALLS TO ENLARGE FEDERAL ROLE AND VOTE FOR SCHOOL AID, 1965

Number of Possible Votes to Enlarge Federal Role	Number of S.D.'s in Group	Number of S.D.'s in Group and Voting for School Aid	Percentage in Group and Voting for School Aid
11–13	18	18	100
9–10	9	7	78
7–8	9	3	33
5–6	12	1	8
3–4	19	2	11
0–2	22	0	0
Total	89	31	35

SOURCE: Compiled from *Congressional Quarterly Weekly Report,* December 3, 1965, pp. 2422–23, and April 2, 1965, pp. 600–601.

Southern Democrats voted for a larger federal role (as defined by *Congressional Quarterly*) on thirteen occasions during the first session of the Eighty-ninth Congress. The table illustrates that a total of 27 southerners voted at least 70 per cent of the time (a minimum of 9 times out of 13 roll calls) for legislation which would enlarge the federal government's role. Included within this "liberal" group of 27 were 25 representatives who also voted for the Education Act of 1965. Thus, a large majority (25 out of 31) of the southern votes for school aid in 1965 were supplied by the more liberal Southern Democrats, those most likely to vote in harmony with their northern colleagues on an issue which included greater federal involvement in the education function and disproportionate assistance to Negro students.

Another characteristic of the group of Southern Democrats who voted for the bill is that about half of them represented highly urban districts. As Table 20 indicates, there were twenty southern congressional districts in 1965 where at least 70 per cent of the population lived in an urban area. Of the 20 representatives from these districts, 15 (or 75 per cent) voted for school aid in 1965 while only 30 per cent and 16 per cent of the representatives from the less urbanized districts supported the legislation. In other words, as was the case with the

Republicans who voted for school aid, the more urban the congressional district the greater the possibility that its representative backed federal aid for education. Certainly the terms of the 1965 bill played a role in attracting the votes of these Republicans and Southern Democrats from urban districts.

TABLE 20

PROPORTION OF SOUTHERN DEMOCRATS VOTING FOR SCHOOL AID,
BY PERCENTAGE OF DISTRICT URBAN, 1965

Percentage of District Urban	Total Districts	Number Voting Yes on Aid	Percentage Voting Yes
High Urban (70–100%)	20	15	75
Medium Urban (40–69%)	37	11	30
Low Urban (0–39%)	32	5	16
Total	89	31	35

SOURCE: Compiled from U.S. Bureau of the Census, *Congressional District Data Book* (Washington: U.S. Government Printing Office, 1963) and *Congressional Quarterly Weekly Report,* April 2, 1965, pp. 600–601.

THE AMERICAN PRESIDENT AS LEGISLATIVE INITIATOR

Inasmuch as the congressional component of the national Democratic party did not initiate but responded to the proposal as drafted by the executive branch, it is necessary to examine the other major result of the 1964 national election: the selection of Lyndon Johnson as President. What kind of leadership, if any, did he contribute to his party's pledge to establish a program of federal assistance for education?

Chief of State, Chief Executive, Supreme Commander of the Armed Forces, Chief Diplomat, Voice of the People, World Leader, Chief of Party, and Chief Legislator are among the many well-known roles or "hats" of the American President.[26] It is important to note, however, as Richard Neustadt has pointed out, that the President must wear all the hats at once since his behavior in any one sphere has implications for all the others.[27] A study of the presidency per se would no doubt emphasize the complex interrelationships among these roles; however, given the nature of this investigation, the discussion will focus on the President as Chief Legislator, or as a source of legislative input.

A variety of factors, including the emergence of America as a world power, the growth of the executive branch, the communications revolu-

[26] Clinton Rossiter, *The American Presidency* (New York: New American Library, 1956), Chapter I.

[27] Richard Neustadt, *Presidential Power* (New York: New American Library, 1960), Preface, VIII.

tion, and the industrialization and urbanization of American society,[28] have contributed to the expansion of the presidential office far beyond the limits conceived by the authors of the Constitution. For example, all the Constitution states on the President's legislative role is that he "shall from time to time give the Congress information of the state of the Union, and recommend to their consideration such measures as he shall judge necessary and expedient . . . ." Yet in modern times the Chief Executive has become the primary initiator of most major bills. Rossiter has suggested that this development is basically due to the increased "complexity of the problems" confronting the nation. He continues by asserting that:

> The President alone is in a political, constitutional, and practical position to provide such leadership, and he is therefore expected, within the limits of constitutional and political propriety, to guide Congress in much of its lawmaking activity.[29]

This dimension of presidential functions requires, among other things, the making of decisions concerning legislative priorities. Given the limits of time and energy, the President is faced with the task of deciding which problems, among the vast array existing in the nation and the world, he will attempt to treat and which of his proposals are most vital and therefore require his utmost attention.

The linkage between the perennial problem of priorities and federal school aid is suggested by one student of the aid movement who concludes his analysis by constructing an ideal pattern that must exist if a federal aid bill is to be realized. The primary part of this pattern is a President who is more than merely in favor of federal aid for education, "the President would have to be for it in a broad and comprehensive way, and feverishly enough to give it a top priority in his program."[30] To what extent has school aid received such attention; how willing have postwar Presidents been to lend substantial amounts of prestige and persuasion to the cause of federal aid to education? More specifically, how does President Johnson's commitment to federal school aid compare with that of other Presidents, and what was his part in the proponent victory of 1965?

A consideration of comparative presidential views on and attention to school aid plus presidential ability to influence Congress is necessary to fashion adequate answers to these questions. The latter, of course, is easier said than done. Although attempts have been made to compare and

---

[28] For a discussion of these factors see Nelson Polsby, *Congress and the Presidency* (Englewood Cliffs: Prentice-Hall, Inc., 1964), pp. 12–14.

[29] Rossiter, *The American Presidency*, p. 19.

[30] Bendiner, *Obstacle Course on Capitol Hill*, p. 192.

rank the effectiveness of Presidents,[31] one must recognize that the many variables involved make such comparisons only suggestive.

POSTWAR PRESIDENTS AND FEDERAL AID TO EDUCATION

President Harry S Truman, as noted earlier, was elected on a platform that endorsed federal aid to education, and he made it part of his Fair Deal program which was presented to the Eighty-first Congress. In his State of the Union Message of 1949 he stated:

> We are not yet assuring all the children of our nation the opportunity of receiving the basic education which is necessary to a strong democracy. . . . I cannot repeat too strongly my desire for prompt federal financial aid to the states to help them operate and maintain their school systems.[32]

Although a school-aid bill did pass the Senate during that year, the House proposal launched a bitter controversy over parochial school aid that has only been matched by the 1961 conflict. Subcommittee Chairman Graham A. Barden (Democrat, North Carolina) introduced a bill authorizing grants of $300 million annually but restricting the aid to public schools. When the bill created a deadlock over aid to private schools at the full committee level, the issue gained nationwide attention as Francis Cardinal Spellman and Mrs. Eleanor Roosevelt became involved in a public conflict over the dispute.

Although President Truman did not engage in a major effort to resolve the impasse, the intensity of the conflict makes it doubtful that action on his part would have settled the question. Additionally, his attention to school aid was necessarily limited because other aspects of his domestic program, such as his compulsory health insurance plan, the establishment of a new executive Department of Health, Education, and Security, the repeal of the Taft-Hartley Act, and abolishment of the poll tax, were all experiencing difficulties. Consequently, although President Truman favored federal assistance, his difficulties with his over-all domestic program, and the heated religious conflict surrounding the aid issue during his term, afforded him little opportunity to assume a leadership role in federal aid for education.

A forecast of the fate awaiting federal aid under President Eisenhower was also revealed during the 1949 action. As president of Columbia

---

[31] See, for example, Arthur M. Schlesinger, Sr., *Paths to the Present* (New York: Macmillan Company, 1949), pp. 93–111, and Arthur M. Schlesinger, "Our Presidents: A Rating by 75 Historians," *The New York Times Magazine,* July 29, 1962, p. 12.

[32] *Public Papers of the Presidents of the United States, Harry S. Truman, 1949* (Washington: U.S. Government Printing Office, 1960), p. 5.

University, Dwight Eisenhower sent a letter to the House Subcommittee on Education expressing approval of federal school aid to only those areas where the tax-paying potential could not provide adequate education. He also remarked:

> I would flatly oppose any grant by the Federal Government to all states in the Union for educational purposes. . . . Unless we are careful even the great and necessary educational processes in our country will become yet another vehicle by which the believer in paternalism, if not outright socialism, will gain still additional power for the central government.[33]

With his concept of federal aid, and given the fact that he was elected on a platform clearly opposing aid to education, it is not surprising that President Eisenhower was opposed to school aid during his first term. His reservations were expressed in his budget message of January 21, 1954, when he stated:

> I do not underestimate the difficulties facing the states and communities in attempting to solve the problems created by the great increase in the number of children of school age, the shortage of qualified teachers, and the overcrowding of classrooms. . . . At the same time, I do not accept the simple remedy of Federal intervention.[34]

Among other things he proposed a White House Conference to study education problems, particularly the question of federal involvement, before any congressional action was taken. The White House Conference on Education began in November, 1955, amid charges that it was stacked by those who opposed federal aid. Its eventual endorsement of school aid, however, muffled critics. Subsequently, the Eisenhower adminstration modified its opposition toward aid and proposed a school construction bill in 1956, which unfortunately for the proponents, became entangled with the segregation issue and was defeated on the House floor. One year later a similar proposal was killed in the House by a vote of 208 to 203 (111 Republicans voted against the bill while 77 voted for it) as both Republicans and Democrats charged President Eisenhower with providing less than enthusiastic backing for his own bill. One veteran supporter of education aid in the Senate summarized the sentiments at a later date when he remarked:

> It was what the administration did—or didn't do—that killed the legislation. The truth of the matter was that Eisenhower never wanted Federal aid. I think some of his friends on the golf course must have

---

[33] Quoted in Congressional Quarterly Service, *Federal Role in Education*, p. 19.
[34] *Public Papers of the Presidents of the United States, Dwight D. Eisenhower, 1954* (Washington: U.S. Government Printing Office, 1960), pp. 151–52.

told him that it was creeping socialism. I really do. In 1957, the bill lost in the House by 5 votes. He could have had a bill. A few phone calls to members of Congress, "This is the President of the United States calling Congressman so and so"—and he'd have gotten the votes. If he had called up Charlie Halleck and Joe Martin and said "I want the votes," he could have gotten them. The struggle would never have been as close as it was. He just didn't want a bill. He did nothing and in that situation, inaction meant, "No."[35]

Certainly it is clear that President Eisenhower was anything but "feverishly" in favor of federal aid; his original opposition to the policy and his general budgetary philosophy did not result in a strong presidential effort to initiate such a program.

President Kennedy presented a striking contrast; he made federal aid to education, as noted previously, one of the 1960 campaign issues and a key item of his domestic program. His concern with the question is testified to by Theodore Sorensen, who has written that education was "the one domestic subject that mattered most to John Kennedy. . . . Throughout his campaign and throughout his Presidency, he devoted more time and talks to this single topic than to any other domestic issue."[36]

In his first education message to Congress, President Kennedy requested a program of $2.3 billion in grants for three years to be used for school construction and boosting teachers' salaries, loans to colleges of almost $2.8 billion to be used over a five-year period for construction purposes, and grants of $892 million for four-year federal college scholarships.[37] None of the elementary and secondary school funds would be available to private schools. As the discussion in the preceding chapter pointed out, this provision eventually spelled the doom of the Kennedy aid program. Although the request was repeated in 1962, the intensity of the 1961 fight discouraged both the administration and congressional proponents from making another major effort.

There is little doubt that President Kennedy strongly favored school aid, but his willingness to exert his full resources on Congress to enact a program has been questioned. Hugh Douglas Price has suggested that in the process of weighing the costs involved in the school fight against his total legislative program the President "apparently decided to knuckle under on aid to education." Price's study of the 1961 school-aid action led to the conclusion that: "The President was simply not pre-

[35] Quoted in Munger and Fenno, *National Politics and Federal Aid to Education*, p. 149. Also see *Congressional Quarterly Almanac*, 1957, p. 592.

[36] Sorensen, *Kennedy*, p. 358.

[37] *Public Papers of the Presidents of the United States, John F. Kennedy, 1961* (Washington: U.S. Government Printing Office, 1962), pp. 107–10.

pared to jeopardize his whole legislative program—and perhaps his chances for re-election—by a bitter fight to the death for aid to education."[38] One might add that, had Kennedy decided to do the opposite, there was no guarantee that victory would result. Given the President's campaign pledge on the question of private school aid, the fact that he was the first Catholic President, and the rigidity of the various groups on the issue, there apparently was little room for presidential maneuverability that would have resolved the conflict.

PRESIDENT LYNDON JOHNSON AND FEDERAL SCHOOL AID

The 1964 Democratic landslide not only resulted in a more liberal Congress, it also returned to the White House a President who, like his predecessor, enthusiastically endorsed an expanded federal role in the field of education. President Lyndon Johnson clearly made federal aid to education at all levels one of the paramount features of the Great Society. He repeatedly emphasized that "every child must be encouraged to get as much education as he has the ability to take." In his State of the Union Message on January 4, 1965, he designated educational goals to head the national agenda: "I propose we begin a program in education to insure every American child the fullest development of his mind and skills." His education message of January 12, 1965, reaffirmed this priority:

> Nothing matters more to the future of our country: not our military preparedness, for armed might is worthless if we lack brainpower to build a world of peace; not our productive economy, for we cannot sustain growth without trained manpower; not our democratic system of government, for freedom is fragile if citizens are ignorant . . . [Therefore] we must demand that our schools increase not only the quantity but the quality of America's education. . . . I urge that we now push ahead with the No. 1 business of the American people—the education of our youth in the preschools, elementary and secondary schools, and in the colleges and universities.[39]

With a more than 2-to-1 Democratic majority in Congress, President Johnson wasted little time in moving to convert these words into action. His desire to have the Elementary and Secondary Education Act of 1965 passed and his willingness to exert every available resource to do

---

[38] Price, "Race, Religion, and the Rules Committee," in Westin, *The Uses of Power,* p. 68.

[39] Senate Committee on Labor and Public Welfare, *Elementary and Secondary Education Act of 1965: Background Material with Related Presidential Recommendations,* pp. 12–13.

so have been commented on by friend and foe alike. One official, for instance, who worked in both the Kennedy and Johnson administrations, commented on Johnson's keen interest in the matter in the following way:

> I don't know what other Presidents think and care about but this one really cares about education. With all due respect to Kennedy we never had the cooperation or pressure from the White House like we've had with Johnson. He simply was determined to get this thing through and everyone knew it.

A representative of a major interest group that worked closely with the administration on the bill also praised the President's intimate support: "He supported it to the hilt. If a Congressman wasn't going to vote for the bill, Johnson wanted to know personally who he was and why he wasn't going to vote for it."

On the other hand, opponents of the measure claimed that President Johnson's manner of backing the proposal resulted in railroading the bill through the legislative process and reducing the legislative branch of the national government to a rubber stamp. These accusations stemmed in part from the fact that the President insisted that the bill be processed as quickly as possible and without revision in order to reduce the possibility of repeating a serious religious dispute over the issue. To meet these demands, committee chairmen in both chambers were called upon to hold hearings on Saturdays (almost unheard of early in a congressional session), amendments were strongly resisted by the proponents in committee executive meetings and on the floor, and great pressure was put on the Senate to pass a bill exactly in the same form as the House version to avert the need for a conference, thereby circumventing the House Rules Committee. The dissatisfaction aroused by these procedures, even among supporters of aid, was summarized by Senator Winston Prouty (Republican, Vermont):

> The Constitution of the United States vests legislative power in the Senate and the House of Representatives. Now, by decree of the President of the United States, the Senate is to be shorn of its equal share of that power. This important and complex piece of legislation—on which your committee heard more than 90 witnesses whose testimony filled 6 volumes and more than 3,200 pages—is to pass this body without a dot or comma changed; this by fiat from the Chief Executive. . . .
>
> The intent of the sponsor of this legislation—the President of the United States—is that the Senate passively accept his decree and pass this bill in exactly the form voted upon by the other body. . . .
>
> Today may be the day when the Senate of the United States, after

176 years of greatness, yields to the insistent demand of a Chief Executive its right and duty to perform its true legislative function.[40]

The fact that some may view President Johnson's role in the proceedings as "presidential leadership" and others as "political arm-twisting" is secondary. The primary fact is that he pushed for federal school aid as no other postwar President had, and he was successful. In terms of the presidential dimension of the 1965 school-aid victory,

TABLE 21

PLURALITY OF DEMOCRATIC NATIONAL LEGISLATIVE SEATS
AND PLURALITY OF PRESIDENTIAL VOTE, 1948–64

	Democratic Plurality of Seats			Popular Vote Plurality
	House	Senate	President	
1948	92	12	Truman	2,135,747
1950	36	2		
1952	−8	1	Eisenhower	6,621,242
1954	29	1		
1956	33	2	Eisenhower	9,567,720
1958	128	30		
1960	89	28	Kennedy	112,803
1962	83	36		
1964	155	36	Johnson	15,952,085

SOURCE: Derived from Congress and the Nation (Washington: Congressional Quarterly, Inc., 1965), pp. 63–66.

why was this so; why did President Johnson succeed when all other postwar Presidents had witnessed the defeat of their school-aid proposals?

In addition to the factors discussed in previous chapters, several characteristics unique to President Johnson help to answer this question. His legislative achievements in the field of education must be viewed in the context of his personal interest in this area, his huge victory and the Democratic party's landslide in the 1964 election, his over-all legislative accomplishments, and his much-heralded ability to understand and work with Congress.

The positive congressional response to his programs is explained, in part, by the fact that Johnson was elected by a plurality of almost 16 million votes, the greatest presidential margin in American history. Contrasted, for example, to Kennedy's slight victory (see Table 21), this impressive mandate at the polls provided Johnson with a significant

[40] Congressional Record, April 7, 1965, pp. 7064–65. Also see Roger A. Freeman, "How to Railroad a School Bill," National Review, 17 (May 18, 1965), 419–22, and "Through the Back Door," The Nation, 200 (April 26, 1965), 434.

lever in dealing with Congress. He could convincingly argue, as he did, that the public had clearly endorsed his policy orientations and he was responsible, as was the Congress, for fulfilling the mandate.

Equally important, his personal sweep at the polls was also largely responsible for his party's gain in seats within the legislative branch. Surely the forty-eight representatives who won formerly held Republican districts in the 1964 election were to some extent indebted to Johnson's "coattails" and were expected to support most of the President's legislative requests.[41] As has been pointed out, this increased margin of liberal Democratic representatives furnished the President with a party advantage that certainly lubricated the congressional machine for both his education and noneducation programs. This plurality in popular votes and in party make-up of the legislature was greater for Johnson than for any other postwar President. Consequently the opportunity for enacting a federal school-aid bill, considering his great interest in doing so, was unusually good.

Although a large numerical majority in the legislature may present a President with the opportunity for fulfilling his agenda, it is not axiomatic that large majorities equal great legislative records. Members of the party with a considerable edge are apt to decide that their votes on a particularly sensitive question, such as federal aid to education, are not vital. The argument that "the President really needs you on this one" is much less effective than in the situation where the majority is narrow and every vote is crucial. Therefore, it is quite tempting for those in the majority to subordinate party loyalty when there is a conflict between presidential wishes and constituency opinions or special interest. A large majority carries with it the additional danger that the opposition party and the press will eventually stress the argument that the President is dictating to the legislature. A continuous repetition of this rubber-stamp accusation may pressure members of the majority into rebuffing the President in order to maintain congressional independence and prerogatives.

Both hazards faced President Johnson during the first session of the Eighty-ninth Congress, but as the data included in Table 22 indicate, he was successful in overcoming them. The table shows that of the 469 proposals he submitted to the Congress 321, or 68.4 per cent, were approved—an all-time high since such scores have been systematically kept. Obviously, there are several pitfalls in taking comparative legislative scores too seriously. However, used with caution, these scores do provide at least a rough estimate of how well a President has done with his legislative program and how he compares with other Presidents. In such terms, Johnson would have to rate highly not only for the proportion of proposals approved but for the number put forth for congressional consideration. In fact, if the number of proposals in Table 22 are broken down into those that *Congressional Quarterly* designates as roll call votes which "present clear-cut tests of support," then Johnson's legislative success is the highest attained by any President since *Congressional Quarterly* began its presidential support studies in 1953. Of 274 such roll call votes in the first session of the Eighty-ninth Congress, 93 per

TABLE 22
PRESIDENTIAL LEGISLATIVE SCORES, 1953–65

	Proposals Submitted	Approved by Congress	Approval Score (%)
1954 (Eisenhower)	232	150	64.7
1955	207	96	46.3
1956	225	103	45.7
1957	206	76	36.9
1958	234	110	47.0
1959	238	93	40.8
1960	183	56	30.6
1961 (Kennedy)	355	172	48.4
1962	298	133	44.6
1963	401	109	27.2
1964 (Johnson)	217	125	57.6
1965	469	321	68.4

SOURCE: *Congressional Quarterly Weekly Report,* November 19, 1965, p. 2341.

cent were approved. This percentage was five points higher than President Johnson's 1964 score; it also exceeded the score of 87.1 per cent made by President Kennedy in 1963 and 89 per cent achieved by President Eisenhower in 1953.[42]

Certainly the party majority factor was important in what has been referred to as "unquestionably one of the most glittering records of legislative accomplishment in history,"[43] but, as has already been suggested, the President must be particularly skillful in dealing with a Congress that is characterized by a large party majority. That Lyndon Johnson has been proficient is attested to by the evidence given above and by the reams of newspaper accounts which have utilized every conceivable adjective in describing his ability in handling the presidential job. Few would disagree with the statement of one close observer of the Washington scene that "Mr. Johnson is the most expert politician, the

[41] The seventy-one Democratic freshmen supported the President on 89 per cent of twelve key roll call votes identified by *Congressional Quarterly* and on 83 per cent of the sixty-six roll call votes held by August, 1965. *Congressional Quarterly Weekly Report,* August 27, 1965, p. 1746.

[42] See *Congressional Quarterly Weekly Report,* November 26, 1965, p. 2387.

[43] *The New York Times,* September 5, 1965, p. 44.

most artful accumulator and dispenser of power, and the most dominant personality to sit in the White House since Franklin Roosevelt."[44]

Many personal factors reportedly underlie President Johnson's ability to get his programs through Congress: his long experience in the Congress, his skill in accumulating power and his astuteness in utilizing it, his ability to sense public opinion on an issue,[45] his touch for great timing, and so on. One factor, however, is emphasized repeatedly in the more extensive accounts of this topic: Johnson understands and appreciates the internal workings of Congress and has the greatest reservoir of informal congressional relations of any other recent President, and probably any President in American history. James Reston put it well when he wrote that President Johnson

> . . . accepts the Congressional system the way it is—warts and all. Kennedy was in the Congress, Johnson is of it. He struggled to the top through the system and therefore thinks it's all right. He is not a critic of the elders of the Congress but their companion. He has lived with them for 30 years, spoken for them in their elections, stood up with them at their family weddings and christenings and funerals; drunk whiskey with them in Mr. Sam Rayburn's "board of education" hideaway in the House.[46]

President Johnson's part in the passage of the 1965 Education Act must be viewed as one thread, and a key one, within this general picture of unprecedented presidential influence. His great personal interest in education (it is reported he would like to be known as the "Education President"), the party line-up, and his remarkable talent for dealing with Congress all favored the enactment of a school-aid bill. In addition, it is important to note that Johnson, not being a Catholic, was in a much better position to propose an education bill that included some assistance to nonpublic schools. With the racial issue generally neutralized, he did so and skillfully enough that the one remaining issue with the greatest potential for blocking his proposal did not re-explode.

[44] Tom Wicker, "The Awesome Twosome," *The New York Times Magazine,* January 30, 1966, p. 6.

[45] Press Secretary Bill Moyers, for example, claims that the President has "a great natural gift for knowing, feeling and sensing the mood of the American people. . . . I think he has antennae that give or take one or two degrees, keeps him pretty closely attuned to the problems, moods and attitudes of the people," *The New York Times,* November 1, 1965, p. 3.

[46] James Reston, "What's He Like?" *The New York Times Magazine,* January 17, 1965, p. 8.

V. Alterations Within the Political System

All of the changes examined thus far involve alterations in the environment of the legislative system and constitute, in terms of the framework being utilized in this study, new inputs. One might assume that these alterations would be sufficient to account for the new policy output. Although tempting, it is not a safe assumption. External changes do not automatically bring about innovation in the system and in its policy outputs for the simple reason that the institutional structure of the system is rigged against producing change. The bias against innovation derives from the fact that the proponents of a new policy must win approval from the two House committees; one Senate committee; both legislative bodies; the House Rules Committee a second time if a conference is necessary; the President; and finally, if the policy is to be carried out, the Appropriations Committees. On the other hand, the opponents of innovation need to block a proposal at only one of these hurdles to prevent its realization.

Given this decentralization of power in the congressional system, the opponents of federal school-aid bills have found the internal institutional structure an important advantage in their efforts to defeat proposals. In fact, one student of the history of federal aid to education has interpreted the proponent failure, prior to 1965, as basically a result of the formal institutional structure of Congress. He has written:

> . . . It is plain that sponsors of Federal aid to the schools have again and again been bilked of their prize solely by the mechanical arrangements of the national legislature. That is to say, they have been beaten not because a majority of the Congress decided, after reasonable thought, that the scheme was contrary to the public good, but simply because a minority used the arrangements in question to have its own way . . . a standing committee of the House regularly buried the legislation in the 1940's sometimes by a single vote; riders and tricky maneuvers killed it on the floor throughout the following decade; and

110

since then it has twice been done to death by that peculiar institution, the Committee on Rules.[1]

Although much has been written about the need for institutional reform of the national legislature, it is important to note that the institutional system serves a variety of functions, even for those who often criticize it. It is a known fact, for example, that congressmen have on occasion written to their constituents complaining that the Rules Committee was blocking a piece of legislation and, at the same time, have encouraged members of the Rules Committee to keep the measure from the floor.[2] Consequently, an institutional interpretation of proponent failure must be considered with some reservations since it may tend to cloud the underlying political conflicts surrounding the school-aid issue.

According to the institutional perspective, change in past outcomes can occur if institutional alterations are made which reduce the ability of a powerful few situated at key junctions in the system to block the will of the majority. In other words, change is more likely to come about when the structure is altered to facilitate a more fluid flow of majority wishes. The primary objective here, then, is essentially to describe changes within the system which increased the probability that the 1965 bill would reach the House floor for a vote, since the structural features of that chamber have most often contributed to past proponent failures.

There were three institutional changes made prior to 1965 which were instrumental in paving the way for the eventual passage of the 1965 Education Act. They were: (1) the revision of the party ratio in the House Committee on Education and Labor in 1959; (2) the shift from Graham Barden to Adam Clayton Powell as chairman of that committee in 1961; (3) the temporary expansion of the House Rules Committee in 1961 and its permanent expansion in 1963.

THE HOUSE COMMITTEE ON EDUCATION AND LABOR

In contrast to the Senate, where federal aid bills had been approved in 1948, 1949, 1960, and 1961 before the 1965 enactment, the House of Representatives was a hostile environment for school-aid proposals. Proponents lacked earlier success in the House because they were unable to accomplish the most elementary victory, that is, to muster sufficient

[1] Bendiner, *Obstacle Course on Capitol Hill*, p. 207.
[2] *Ibid.*, p. 155. Also see Howard W. Smith, "In Defense of the House Rules Committee," in Joseph S. Clark (ed.), *Congressional Reform: Problems and Prospects* (New York: Thomas Y. Crowell Company, 1965), pp. 138–50.

strength in the House Committee on Education and Labor to have a bill favorably reported. As Figure 2 indicates, the proponents usually were able to secure committee hearings during the years after World War II;

FIGURE 2

HOUSE ACTION ON FEDERAL AID TO EDUCATION BILLS, 1945–65

Congress and Year	Committee Hearings Held	Reported from Committee	Approved by Rules Committee	Debated on Floor	Passed by House	Conference Held	Signed by President
79th							
1945	———						
1946	– – – –						
80th							
1947	———						
1948	– – – –						
81st							
1949	———						
1950	———						
82nd							
1951							
1952	———						
83rd							
1953							
1954	———						
84th							
1955	——————————						
1956	– – – – – – – – – –	———————					
85th							
1957	——————————————————————						
1958	———						
86th							
1959	——————————						
1960	– – – – – – – – – –	———————————————					
87th							
1961	——————————						
1962	———						
88th							
1963	———						
1964							
89th							
1965	————————————————————————————————————					(none)	———

——— Action taken during session.
– – – – – Action taken in prior session.

however, it was not until 1955 that a bill finally was reported from the committee.

In an attempt to explain this action, Richard Fenno has called attention to several characteristics of the House Committee on Education and Labor which have made consensus building in general difficult and concurrence on the issue of school aid particularly formidable.[3] He notes that "nearly all of its members agree that it is probably the most difficult House committee in which to achieve a consensus and the easiest in which to promote and prolong conflict."[4] The factors underpinning this assessment pertain to the nature of the committee's jurisdiction, the composition of its membership, and its decision-making procedures.

Much of the committee's preoccupation with conflict instead of consensus building results because many of the most controversial and highly partisan domestic issues fall within the committee's jurisdiction. With responsibilities spanning from the Taft-Hartley bill (its first major bill) to the current antipoverty legislation, the Committee on Education and Labor, as one member commented, "is probably the most partisan Committee in the House, because this is where the fundamental philosophical battles are fought."[5] Given such a situation, flexibility is generally lacking and compromise is hard to come by. This was stressed by a former committee member who recalled the federal aid fight during the 1950's: "Some of us were unalterably opposed to Federal aid and some on the other side were just as unalterably in favor of it. . . . There weren't many minds changed by discussion."[6]

However, as Fenno has pointed out, issues alone do not produce conflict; it is the personnel on the committee and their relative perspectives on issues which cause disagreement. In this sense, the composition of the committee's membership is a vital factor, and as Masters has noted:

> The assignment of members to the Education and Labor Committee —with jurisdiction over the explosive issues of school aid, segregation and labor management relations—has called for the most careful attention to the constituencies of applicants. . . . It is no place for a neutral when there are so many belligerents around.[7]

[3] See Chapter V in Munger and Fenno, *National Politics and Federal Aid to Education,* and "The House of Representatives and Federal Aid to Education," in Peabody and Polsby, *New Perspectives on the House of Representatives,* pp. 195–235.

[4] Munger and Fenno, *National Politics and Federal Aid to Education,* p. 109.

[5] Quoted in *ibid.,* p. 110.

[6] *Ibid.*

[7] Nicholas A. Masters, "House Committee Assignment," *American Political Science Review,* LV (June, 1961), 354.

Both political parties recognize this fact and attempt to control the composition of the membership through careful assignment procedures. Democrats have promoted their perspective in the committee by encouraging the appointment of "dependable" liberals—"those who can afford politically to take an outright pro-labor position"[8]—and by limiting the assignment of southerners. Republican party leaders, on

TABLE 23

EDUCATION COMMITTEE MEMBERS FAVORING A LARGER FEDERAL ROLE
COMPARED TO HOUSE AND SENATE AS A WHOLE, 1961 AND 1965

	Mean Percentage of Votes for Larger Federal Role	
	1961	1965
	(10 Roll Calls)	(13 Roll Calls)
All House Democrats	78	79
All House Republicans	12	33
Difference	66	46
Committee Democrats	91	95
Committee Republicans	7	30
Difference	84	65
	(10 Roll Calls)	(12 Roll Calls)
All Senate Democrats	67	82
All Senate Republicans	32	46
Difference	35	36
Committee Democrats	90	99
Committee Republicans	52	50
Difference	38	49

SOURCE: *Congressional Quarterly Weekly Report,* October 20, 1961, pp. 1751–63 and December 3, 1965, pp. 2417–20.

the other hand, protect their influence in the committee by assigning to it those who are not moderate on labor-management issues but strongly pro-management.[9]

The assignment practices tend to accentuate the philosophical and partisan division among members resulting from the issues raised by the committee's jurisdiction. The relative intensity of this split is reflected by the data included in Table 23, which compares the ideological

[8] *Ibid.*

[9] This stress by both parties on appointing members according to their views on labor, not education, is another factor which influenced the lack of consensus on the school-aid issue.

differences between Democrats and Republicans in the House as a whole and to the same variations in the Senate. These differences are derived from a series of roll call votes selected by *Congressional Quarterly* in 1961 and 1965 to distinguish, as noted earlier, those congressmen who support a larger federal role in domestic affairs (e.g., liberals) from those who are opposed to a larger federal role (e.g., conservatives). The table shows the mean percentage of each group's vote for expanded federal involvement.

The results of both the 1961 and 1965 analyses indicate that the ideological variation within the House committee was greater than the disagreement between the opposing party members on the same issues in the House as a whole. In both instances the mean percentage difference between Education Committee Democrats and Republicans was about 20 per cent greater than between all House Democrats and Republicans, although the Republican percentage increased significantly during the four-year period.

The pattern in the Senate was quite different. The 1961 variation in voting behavior along party lines between Senate Education Committee members and all senators was small. Additionally, the convergence of views was more apparent in the Senate committee where both Democrats and Republicans indicated a greater willingness to support enlarged federal activity than their respective counterparts in the entire Senate. This pattern at the committee level contributes to the favorable action that federal aid proposals have received in the Senate. In contrast to this relative agreement in the Senate committee, Democrats on the House committee voted more liberally during both periods than did all House Democrats, whereas Republicans on the committee voted more conservatively than did all House Republicans. This fact illustrates the basic discordance in the House committee and underlies the past difficulties faced by school-aid proponents in guiding legislation through the House.

The combination of jurisdictional and membership characteristics of the House Committee on Education and Labor obviously influenced the nature of the committee's decision-making procedures. Given these characteristics, it is not surprising that the committee's style of decision-making does not emphasize accommodation and compromise. In fact, Fenno has commented: "It tends to function in a fiercely competitive style in which the techniques are those of naked power and the decision goes to whoever can command a simple majority in a showdown vote."[10] The informal norms which advance committee integration, such as

[10] Munger and Fenno, *National Politics and Federal Aid to Education*, p. 117.

mutual respect between members of opposite parties, have not developed to the extent they have in other committees.[11] This trait is exemplified by an exchange during the 1965 subcommittee hearings among Chairman Adam Clayton Powell of the full committee, Representative William D. Ford (Democrat, Michigan), and Representative Goodell:

> CHAIRMAN POWELL: Will the gentleman yield?
>
> MR. GOODELL: I have had enough with debating with the other side of the committee. I would like to hear the panel answer some questions.
>
> MR. FORD: I may observe I have been here since 9:30 and have not had a chance to ask any questions.
>
> MR. GOODELL: You asked one earlier and you will have a chance. This is the first Republican question we have had here.
>
> CHAIRMAN POWELL: The gentleman from New York has 1 more minute under the 5-minute rule (which was not observed up to this point in the hearings).
>
> MR. GOODELL: Mr. Chairman, I serve notice, then, if any more speeches are to be delivered in this subcommittee, I will object at the end of 5 minutes under the 5-minute rule. . . . You have more power and you will suppress the minority, but you will hear from us.[12]

The decision-making environment in which the House Education Committee functioned magnifies the significance of the ratio of Democrats to Republicans on the committee. If the possibilities for cooperation and compromise are limited then decisions are indeed an outcome of naked power, and those with the votes rule. In this respect, the sweeping Democratic congressional victory of 1958 and the consequent alteration of the committee's party ratio to produce twenty Democrats to ten Republicans in 1959 instead of the previous line-up of seventeen Democrats to thirteen Republicans constitutes one of the key institutional changes of the federal aid movement.

In 1959, liberal committee members claimed that in past sessions the old ratio allowed the alliance of the Republicans with Chairman Graham A. Barden (Democrat, North Carolina) and Phil M. Landrum (Democrat, Georgia) to bring about a 15–15 voting split, thus blocking action on education aid as well as anti-corruption labor legislation and revisions of the Taft-Hartley Act.[13] Until 1955, this conservative coali-

---

[11] See, for example, Richard F. Fenno, Jr., "The House Appropriations Committee as a Political System: The Problems of Integration," *American Political Science Review* (June, 1962), 310–24.

[12] House Committee on Education and Labor, *Aid to Elementary and Secondary Education*, pp. 596–97.

[13] *Congressional Quarterly Weekly Report,* January 23, 1959, p. 101.

tion permitted the opponents of federal aid[14] to bottle up proposals at the committee level; then the Eisenhower administration presented a program, and the Eisenhower-oriented Republicans on the committee joined the majority of the Democrats to report the bill out. The latter alignment was responsible for reporting bills out in 1956 and 1957; however, it was dissolved in 1958 when President Eisenhower withdrew his support for federal aid. Then the old coalition again stalled the proposal in committee. The adoption of a new two-to-one ratio and the appointment of five "liberal" Democratic freshmen in 1959 strengthened the position of committee liberals and gave them a dominant majority.[15] Since the alteration in committee size was made, the support for federal aid within the committee has been essentially an all-Democratic majority (one Republican joined the Democrats in 1960 and two in 1965, although they did not affect the results) which has been able to process bills through the committee stage whenever earnest administration requests were made. In 1965 the federal aid bill was reported out of committee by the twenty-one Democrats who were joined by Republicans Ogden Reid and Alphonzo Bell. Had the 1959 revision not been accomplished, committee treatment of the 1965 proposal probably would have been more rugged.

HOUSE COMMITTEE LEADERSHIP

Another modification in the congressional system which facilitated the task of advancing school-aid proposals through the House Education Committee was the change from Graham Barden to Adam Clayton Powell as chairman of the committee in 1961. The importance of this change in leadership stems from the powers allocated to committee chairmen in the national legislature.

Committee chairmen have at their disposal a wide assortment of formal and informal powers that permit them to exert a strong influence on the fate of legislation under their jurisdiction. The chairman, for example, controls the agenda of his committee and schedules hearings on those bills, among the many pending, which he feels are most important. He determines the work load by organizing subcommittees, appointing their chairmen, and establishing their jurisdictions. In fact, he may create special subcommittees instead of standing subcommittees (who generally have more autonomy) to give himself even greater

[14] On some occasions those members who generally favored aid also voted against specific bills in committee because of the lack of aid to nonpublic schools or because of the allocation formula.

[15] The five new Democrats were Roman C. Pucinski (Ill.), Dominick V. Daniels (N.J.), John Brademas (Ind.), Robert Giamo (Conn.), and James G. O'Hara (Mich.).

leverage. He also makes the vital decisions concerning when and how long the committee will meet, whether there is a quorum, who will be heard from and for how long, and what the size and competence of the committee's staff will be. Additionally, the chairman manages committee bills on the floor and usually sits on conference committees when legislation from his committee is under consideration.

Graham Barden, during his eight-year tenure (1951–52 and 1955–60) as chairman of the House Committee on Education and Labor, utilized every one of these powers to bury the school-aid proposals before his committee. Fenno, for example, has written that Barden "worked tirelessly to defeat federal aid legislation."[16] Barden has been described as a master at using delaying tactics to forestall action by his committee. One Democratic member of the committee commented:

> He never shut any one up. He'd let you talk yourself around the clock and in circles if you would. One year, he brought in 92 witnesses from the Chamber of Commerce on the school bill and was going to let them all talk.[17]

Another favorite delaying tactic employed by Barden was his authority to halt committee meetings by declaring the absence of a quorum. Even after the 1959 ratio alteration he was able to exercise this prerogative to defer committee business. When liberals on the committee attempted to hold sessions without him, but with the necessary quorum, "Barden would come, look around and say, 'I see there's no quorum present,' bang his gavel and it would be all over."[18]

Barden also used a host of other tactics which weighed against any favorable action on school aid by his committee. Among other things, he refused to establish a regular meeting day for the committee; would not create standing subcommittees with permanent areas of jurisdiction; declined to place a time limit on the questioning of witnesses during hearings; kept the committee's staff small and of low quality; and in 1956, when a school-aid bill was reported from the committee, he demanded the right to manage the floor debate and allocated a disproportionate amount of time to the opponents of the bill.

The proponents of federal aid to education, and of liberal legislation in general, were presented with an unexpected treat on January 22, 1960. On that day Chairman Barden, at the age of sixty-three,

---

16 Munger and Fenno, *National Politics and Federal Aid to Education,* p. 122. As a subcommittee chairman in 1949 Barden initiated the bill and added much of the subsequent fuel to the religious conflict which surrounded the issue during that period.

17 *Ibid.*

18 *Ibid.,* p. 123.

announced to the surprise of House leaders, including Speaker Sam Rayburn, that he was not going to seek election to a fourteenth term but "was going home and take it easy."[19] Although liberals may have uttered a sigh of relief at this news, it immediately became apparent that the notification had a double edge: Barden would no longer be chairman of the House Committee on Education and Labor; but in all probability Adam Clayton Powell, next in seniority, would be heir to the throne.

Powell's well-publicized conduct as a congressman of high absenteeism, high and careless spending of public money, and difficulties with the Internal Revenue, among other things, earned him the reputation (outside his Harlem district) of being irresponsible.[20] In fact, the prospect that Powell would become the new chairman renewed the longtime proposal to divide the committee in two. Under such a change, Powell would be chairman of a new labor committee while Representative Cleveland Bailey (Democrat, West Virginia), who had a number of hot brushes with Powell over the issue of school aid and segregation, would be the chairman of the education committee. Powell, however, made it clear that he would by no means be agreeable to such a modification and indicated that Speaker Rayburn had promised him the position as chairman of the full committee.[21] At a news conference Powell pledged a more liberal and effective committee and indicated that he would no longer press for his anti-segregation amendment to school-aid bills if the committee's majority did not support him:

> I don't think Mr. Barden had the friendship and rapport that I have with these men. Mr. Barden is a dogmatic man with set views against which Young Turks on both sides of the House were rebelling. I'm not going to be anti anybody or anything in Committee. If something like segregation came up, I would accept the committee majority and, if need be, fight it down on the floor of the House.[22]

Soon after the Democratic victory in the fall of 1960, Powell indicated that the committee, in contrast to the past, would be organized for action. Although it was nearly two months before the Eighty-seventh

[19] *The New York Times,* January 23, 1960, p. 1. Also see "Bottleneck in Congress Retires," *Business Week,* January 30, 1960, p. 93.

[20] See, for example, *The New York Times* editorial of January 26, 1960, on Powell's ability to be chairman of the committee. For background on Powell's political "style" see James Q. Wilson, "Two Negro Politicians: An Interpretation," *Midwest Journal of Political Science,* IV (November, 1960), 346–69.

[21] The following day Rayburn announced that the assignment probably would be made "in the natural way" if the Democrats won the election—meaning Powell would be chairman since he had the seniority. *The New York Times,* January 24, 1960, p. 1.

[22] *The New York Times,* January 23, 1960, p. 11.

Congress convened he made assignments to all the majority members of the committee and set them to work for the coming session. He also predicted that the committee would approve bills on minimum wages and federal aid to education within a month after the Congress began its session.[23]

Although the Kennedy education bills were reported from committee in 1961, the controversy over parochial schools, as was discussed earlier, eventually doomed them. This occurred through no fault of Chairman Powell, who dropped his perennial segregation amendment and advocated compromise by suggesting limited parochial assistance to resolve the impasse.

On minimum-wage legislation Powell demonstrated a similar willingness to take positive action. Shortly after the administration submitted its minimum-wage proposal he instructed a subcommittee to consider its legislation and to hold no more than three days of hearings. This was in sharp contrast to the four months of hearings held the year before when Barden was chairman of the committee.[24] On May 3, 1961, the House finally passed a compromise wage bill (230 to 196), and several of Powell's colleagues admitted that he had exhibited unexpected skill during conference hearings and in pushing the compromise legislation through the House. One member of his committee, Edith Green, expressed the observation, "He sees this as the great challenge of his life. He wants to be an outstanding chairman."[25]

Additional evidence indicates that Powell saw the committee as an instrument of action rather than inaction. In contrast to procedures under Barden, Powell instituted such practices as an antifilibuster rule, which may be used to prevent members from talking more than five minutes in full committee during the discussion of bills, and has doubled the size of the staff that served under Barden in his effort to speed up the committee's work. Indeed, in his reorganization of the committee he reportedly considered installing a new intercommunication system in his office that would enable him to participate *in absentia* in subcommittee sessions by cutting in with, "This is your chairman speaking. . . ."[26]

Certainly there were many who continued to have grave reservations about Powell's suitability to be a congressman, let alone the chairman of a key domestic committee. His widely publicized jaunts to foreign countries and a New York City lawsuit against him provided constant fuel

23 *The New York Times,* November 12, 1960, p. 11.
24 See Paul Duke, "A New Role for Mr. Powell," *The Reporter,* September 28, 1961, pp. 30–32.
25 *Ibid.,* p. 31.
26 *Ibid.,* p. 32. Also see Murray Kempton, "Adam Powell: The Ocelot of the House of Representatives," *New Republic,* 148 (May 25, 1963), 10–13.

for such accusations. However, if one assesses Powell strictly on his willingness and ability to process liberal legislation through the House Committee on Education and Labor, particularly federal aid bills, it is clear that he was more efficient than Barden.

The part he played in the passage of the 1965 Education Act is a good example of this appraisal. Prior to the first session of the Eighty-ninth Congress, Chairman Powell indicated that federal school aid would be a top priority item in his committee and reaffirmed his pledge not to entangle school aid with segregation. Noting the Democratic majorities in both houses, Powell said, "If we don't get Federal aid to education in this Congress, we might as well forget all about it for another generation."[27]

President Johnson delivered his education message on January 12; ten days later Powell had his subcommittee conducting hearings on the bill. The hearings lasted from January 22 to February 2; by February 5 the subcommittee cleared the bill and reported it to the full committee, all in record time. Action occurred at such a fast pace that some individuals and groups accused Powell of attempting to "rush through" the public hearings on the President's program before the public became acquainted with the provisions of the bill.[28] However, Powell once again reminded those who might have forgotten that he knew how to be unscrupulous in his manipulation of power. While the administration was waiting for action by the full committee, it was disclosed that Powell was stalling by refusing to call executive sessions on the bill. It became apparent that this action was taken in response to the possibility that his request for committee operating funds might be trimmed; if he did not get the committee budget he wanted, the school-aid bill would gather dust. He made it clear that this was true by stating, after the appropriation was made:

> I consider the Committee on Education and Labor the most important committee on domestic legislation in Congress. I held up everything until I got the money I needed to operate the committee.
>
> I have informed the White House that I will do everything I can to get it through the committee this week if we have to meet all day every day, including Saturday, provided we can hold a quorum on Saturday.[29]

Consequently, Powell scheduled the full committee to meet that Thursday, Friday, and Saturday to approve the bill. However, on Saturday six Democrats joined the commitee's ten Republicans to adjourn the meeting

---

[27] *The New York Times,* December 24, 1964, p. 10.
[28] See, for example, the statement made by Dr. Joachim Prinz, president of the American Jewish Congress, *The New York Times,* January 22, 1965, p. 23.
[29] Quoted in *The New York Times,* February 25, 1965, p. 16.

suddenly by a vote of 16 to 15, thus reportedly preventing Powell from fulfilling his promise to the White House to have the bill approved by the end of the week.[30] The bill, however, was reported by the full committee the following Tuesday, March 2, less than two months after the president had sent it to the House. This speedy and favorable treatment must be credited, to a large extent, to Adam Clayton Powell, who apparently gained some grudging respect from his colleagues for his talent at getting things done. One reporter noted that the school-aid action "illustrates what many Congressmen see as one of the representative's chief redeeming virtues: his ability to run the committee efficiently, processing large amounts of significant and complicated legislation . . ."[31]

THE HOUSE RULES COMMITTEE AND FEDERAL AID TO EDUCATION

The two internal alterations to the legislative system discussed thus far unquestionably enhanced the possibilities of securing favorable action on federal aid legislation by the Education Committee. The shift in party ratio and the ascent of Powell to the chairmanship meant that major liberal legislation would be blocked by this committee only under unusual circumstances. However, even if school-aid proponents had successfully vaulted this hurdle, they were confronted with another barrier: the House Rules Committee, where aid-to-education bills were killed in 1959, 1960, and 1961.

As noted earlier, the Rules Committee functions as the intervening structure in the House between the committees and the floor. It is charged with the responsibility of determining which committee-approved measures will be debated, and under what conditions, on the House floor. Its influence is described by one political scientist in the following manner:

> The base of the Committee's power consists in its opportunities to give or withhold hearings for rules, to give or withhold rules, to trade a change in the bill for a rule, to permit or forbid amendments and set the length of debate, to take advantage of time constraints near the end of a session, to arbitrate differences between legislative committees, and to initiate action in the absence of legislative committee decisions. Its means of power are the actual exercise of these opportunities, plus the delay, threat, or anticipation of their exercise.[32]

[30] *The New York Times,* February 28, 1965, p. 45.
[31] Warren Weaver, Jr., "Powell: Man and Image," *The New York Times,* February 28, 1965, Part IV, p. 4. Apparently this ability and willingness on Powell's part to run the committee efficiently did not extend into the second session of the Eighty-ninth Congress. In September, 1966, the members of his committee banded together to strip him of several powers for his alleged mismanagement and negligence of committee work.
[32] James A. Robinson, *The House Rules Committee* (Indianapolis: The Bobbs-Merrill Company, Inc., 1963), p. 21.

It is not these powers alone, but the utilization of them by a bipartisan conservative alignment to block "liberal" legislation which has been the source of conflict surrounding the appropriate functioning of the Rules Committee. The committee was first taken over by such an alliance in 1937 when a group of dissident Democrats joined the conservative Republicans on the committee to oppose much of President Franklin Roosevelt's legislative program. Between that time and 1961, except for the Republican Eightieth and Eighty-third Congresses, the Rules Committee generally was dominated by this bloc, although Speaker Rayburn occasionally was able to pry loose a crucially needed vote or two through his relationship with Minority Leader Joe Martin.[33]

In 1955 Howard Smith assumed the chairmanship of the committee. His skill at using his position and the powers of the committee to keep close rein over the kind of legislation emerging from the House has become almost legendary. One of his colleagues described his political skill in the following manner:

> One of the interesting things is to watch the way he plays all these different things the way a great conductor conducts an orchestra . . . on an economic issue, or a welfare issue . . . let's say there are five or six of them, he'll play them as carefully as he can and very skillfully to kill as many as possible, but if he has to knuckle under in order to get "X" by going along with "A" he will. It's really magnificent skill.[34]

In a manner similar to Barden, Smith used a variety of techniques to discourage legislation he did not favor. If, for example, legislation was pending which he found objectionable, it was not unusual for him to delay for long periods of time the convening of his committee. The story is told that:

> In August, 1957, he vanished from Washington, leaving his committee without the power to call itself to order, while the civil rights bill gathered dust in its files. Word seeped back from Virginia that Judge Smith had gone to inspect a barn that had burned on his nearby dairy farm.
>
> "I knew Howard Smith would do most anything to block a civil rights bill, but I never suspected he would resort to arson," Speaker Rayburn quipped, somewhat wryly.[35]

---

[33] *Ibid.;* also see Milton C. Cummings, Jr., and Robert L. Peabody, "The Decision to Enlarge the Committee on Rules: An Analysis of the 1961 Vote," in Peabody and Polsby, *New Perspectives on the House of Representatives,* p. 170.

[34] Congressman Richard Bolling on CBS Reports, "The Keeper of the Rules: Congressman Smith and the New Frontier," CBS-TV, January 19, 1961, quoted in Nelson Polsby, *Congress and the Presidency,* p. 73.

[35] Wicker, *The New York Times Magazine,* August 7, 1960, p. 15.

If matters eventually came to a vote, Chairman Smith and William Colmer, a Mississippi Democrat, consistently aligned themselves with the four Republican members of the committee to produce a 6-to-6 tie vote, thus denying the rule.

Dissatisfaction with the situation gained momentum following the 1958 Democratic congressional sweep. Anxious to build a liberal legislative record to campaign on in the 1960 election, a group of Democrats who constituted the Democratic Study Group went to Speaker Rayburn early in 1959 and requested that something be done about the Rules Committee. Counting on his informal relationship with Minority Leader Martin to produce the vital moderate Republican votes to override Smith and Colmer on key issues, Rayburn assured the group that measures would not be bottled up in the Rules Committee. However, shortly after this commitment was made, Martin was defeated as the Republican leader by Charles Halleck in a surprise vote 74 to 70.[36] Furthermore, Halleck replaced two Republicans on the Rules Committee with two more conservative members; consequently the Democratic liberals and leadership saw many of the bills they favored strongly stalled or buried in the committee.[37]

Among the House bills not granted a rule in 1959 was the Murray-Metcalf education bill (H.R. 22), which would have authorized $1.1 billion a year for a four-year period to be used for school construction and teachers' salaries. School-aid supporters were able to secure Education Committee approval by a vote of 18 to 12 (Barden and Landrum voted with the ten Republicans); but they were unable to generate enough pressure to move the proposal through the Rules Committee, where the bill was lodged from June to the end of the session. There is evidence to indicate that the proponents actually did not expect approval of the bill but were interested in spotlighting the obstructive posture of the Rules Committee. One of the bill's coauthors commented:

> We got that bill out of Committee and we knew it didn't stand a chance of getting through the Rules Committee, but we just let it sit there. It put a few feet to fire. We got enough pressure built up so that the next year when we came back with a construction bill we got one extra vote and got it through the Rules Committee.[38]

During the 1960 session the Senate passed an education bill that had been introduced the previous year by Senator Pat McNamara (Democrat,

---

[36] Robinson, *The House Rules Committee*, p. 72.

[37] Ivan Henderaker, "From the 86th to the 87th Congress: Controversy over 'Majority Rule,'" in *American Government Annual, 1961–1962* (New York: Holt, Rinehart & Winston, 1961), pp. 76–98.

[38] Munger and Fenno, *National Politics and Federal Aid to Education*, p. 134.

Michigan). The bill provided an authorization of $1.8 billion for school construction and teachers' salaries, the funds to be distributed in such a manner that the poorer states would receive more money than the wealthier ones.

The House bill provided for construction only and did not include an equalization formula. The proposal was passed by the House Committee on Education and Labor by a vote of 19 to 11; on March 25 it was sent to the Rules Committee, where nothing happened to it until the middle of May. Impatient over the long delay in Rules, the sponsors of school aid decided to use Calendar Wednesday (which had been used successfully to pass the Area Redevelopment bill earlier) to bring the bill to the House floor. However, twenty-four hours before the deadline, Chairman Smith "made it known that he would hold a hearing on the education bill on Thursday morning (May 19) if plans for Calendar Wednesday were dropped."[39]

Rather than encourage the use of Calendar Wednesday, thus under-cutting the influence of the Rules Committee, Smith presumably decided that it would be wise for the committee members to make the decision. It soon became apparent that Smith had resisted putting the issue to a vote because the coalition that blocked much legislation with a 6-to-6 tie would be temporarily broken. This development resulted from the fact that B. Carroll Reece, a Republican from Tennessee, was reportedly under considerable fire from his financially needy constituents, who were aware that the Rules Committee had blocked school aid the previous year. Consequently, the constituents pressed Reece to support the 1960 education bill, and he had pledged to do so.[40] Therefore, on May 19 the bill received a rule to proceed to the floor by a vote of 7 to 5 (see Table 24).

Action on the floor eventually resulted in House approval of a general school-aid bill for the first time in American history. Bolstered by the Democratic victory in 1958, the pro-aid forces were able to fashion a 206-to-189 vote for passage. However, the victory was gained at the cost of attaching the Powell amendment to the bill. Despite the pleas of Democratic floor leaders, one hundred Northern and Western Democrats, who were facing a fall election, voted for the Civil Rights proposition. They were joined by seventy-seven Republicans who subsequently turned around and voted against final passage. The inclusion of the Powell amendment, as it turned out, eventually doomed the legislation.[41]

Since the House version differed from the Senate's education bill, a

[39] Bendiner, *Obstacle Course on Capitol Hill*, p. 166.
[40] *Ibid.*
[41] *Congressional Quarterly Weekly Report*, May 27, 1960, pp. 919–20.

conference was necessary to work out the appropriate adjustments. Unless unanimous consent is granted for such a conference, it is necessary to secure a special rule from the Rules Committee; this became necessary when Representative August Johansen (Republican, Michi-

TABLE 24

VOTES IN RULES COMMITTEE TO EXPEDITE FEDERAL AID LEGISLATION, 1960–65

	1960 1st Vote	1960 2nd Vote	1961 1st Vote	1961 2nd Vote	1965 Vote
DEMOCRATS					
Smith (Va.)	N	N	N	N	N
Colmer (Miss.)	N	N	N	N	N
Madden (Ind.)	Y	Y	Y	Y	Y
Delaney (N.Y.)	Y	Y	N	N	Y
Trimble (Ark.)	Y	N	Y	Y	Y
Thornberry (Tex.)	Y	Y	Y	Y	
Bolling (Mo.)	Y	Y	Y	Y	Y
O'Neill (Mass.)	Y	Y	N	Y	Y
Elliott (Ala.)			Y	Y	
Sisk (Cal.)			Y	Y	Y
Young (Tex.)					Y
Pepper (Fla.)					Y
REPUBLICANS					
Allen (Ill.)	N	N			
Brown (Ohio)	N	N	N	N	N
Reece (Tenn.)	Y	N			
Budge (Ida.)	N	N			
St. George (N.Y.)			N	N	
Smith (Cal.)			N	N	N
Hoffman (Ill.)			N	N	
Avery (Kan.)			N	N	
Anderson (Ill.)					N
Martin (Neb.)					N
Quillen (Tenn.)					N
Totals	Y-7 N-5	Y-5 N-7	Y-6 N-9	Y-7 N-8	Y-8 N-7

Y = Yes Vote
N = No Vote

gan) objected. The House Committee on Rules while meeting in executive session on June 22 refused by a 7-to-5 vote to send the legislation to conference.

Representatives James W. Trimble (Democrat, Arkansas) and B. Carroll Reece, both of whom voted to expedite the measure on May 19, reversed their positions and voted against it on June 22. It was reported that Trimble, a supporter of federal aid, found it politically hazardous to promote a bill containing an anti-segregation clause, while Reece no longer felt obligated to vote against his convictions since he had fulfilled his original pledge. Subsequently, little was done to alter the situation between June 22 and September 1, when Congress adjourned. Apparently, Republicans were relieved that President Eisenhower would not have to make a choice between vetoing an education bill in an election year and signing a bill he had denounced publicly. Many liberal Democrats, on the other hand, were more interested in a campaign issue than pushing for a conference which undoubtedly would result in deleting the teachers' salaries from the bill. One of the five Democrats on the Rules Committee who voted for the conference indicated later why they did not fight for a turnabout: "We were planning a full-scale attack on the power of the Committee and we felt that the worse it looked, the better."[42]

After the 1960 election, President-elect Kennedy and his fellow liberal Democrats realized that confrontation with the Rules Committee was necessary. Kennedy felt that, unless something was done to break the conservative block, "nothing controversial would come to the floor of the Congress. Our whole program would be emasculated."[43] However, Kennedy also knew that the initiative for change must come from the House of Representatives instead of from the White House; consequently, Speaker Sam Rayburn would be largely responsible for deciding how to handle the Rules Committee.[44]

The choices open to the Speaker all involved a basic decision concerning whether a change should be made to dilute the institutional power of the committee or to alter its political balance without tampering with its authority. For example, an attempt could be made to reinstitute the "twenty-one-day rule"[45] used in 1949, to reduce the number of names

[42] This statement of Representative Richard Bolling was quoted by Bendiner, *Obstacle Course on Capitol Hill,* p. 171.

[43] Quoted in Sorensen, *Kennedy,* p. 340. On August 26, 1960, eleven members rose on the House floor to denounce the Rules Committee and demand reform. *Congressional Record,* August 26, 1960, pp. 16698–706.

[44] There are several informative studies of this topic. See: Price, "Race, Religion and the Rules Committee," in Westin, *The Uses of Power,* pp. 1–73; Cummings and Peabody, "The Decision to Enlarge the Committee on Rules," in Peabody and Polsby, *New Perspectives on the House of Representatives;* Robert Peabody, "The Enlarged Rules Committee," in the same volume; Robinson, *The House Rules Committee;* Neil MacNeil, *The Forge of Democracy* (New York: David McKay Company, 1963), pp. 410–48; and William R. MacKaye, *A New Coalition Takes Control: The House Rules Committee Fight of 1961* (New York: McGraw-Hill Book Co., 1963).

[45] The rule made it possible for the Speaker of the House to allow a committee chairman to submit a bill for House consideration if the Rules Committee had failed to take action on it for twenty-one days.

required for a discharge petition, to restrict the powers of the chairman, or to limit the jurisdiction of the committee. On the other hand, the Speaker could opt for retaining a strong Rules Committee by changing the composition of the membership, thus harnessing the committee's power to work for the will of the majority. This could be done in two ways. First, the decision could be made among Democrats (as was suggested by the Democratic Study Group) by removing Representative William Colmer from the committee on grounds that he had campaigned against the Democratic party in the previous election.[46] Then he could be replaced by a "loyal" Democrat who would create a 7-to-5 "liberal" majority. Second, the entire House could be called upon to enlarge the Rules Committee from twelve to fifteen members. The two-to-one ratio of majority to minority could be maintained by allowing the Republicans to add one member while the Democrats added two. Since Halleck could be expected to add a conservative and Rayburn two "liberal" Democrats (one southern to maintain the balance on civil rights), this alteration would result in an 8-to-7 line-up that would ordinarily report "liberal" legislation, except civil rights which would need Republican support on the committee.

After reportedly feeling Smith out and not finding him agreeable to any change, Rayburn indicated that he leaned, though reluctantly, toward replacing Colmer. This approach immediately triggered strong resistance, particularly from those committed to the seniority system. It was pointed out that others had not been chastised for similar action in the past. Adam Clayton Powell, for example, had supported Eisenhower in 1956 but retained his place in the party hierarchy. It was noted also that this action was likely to alienate Southern Democrats to the point where they would join Republicans on the floor of the House, thus endangering the President's program even if it were able to proceed through Rules.[47]

Consequently, Rayburn announced later that he favored an enlarged Rules Committee as the most "painless" way out of the circumstance.[48] Since this decision meant that the entire House would be involved in the outcome, Rayburn needed considerable southern support and votes from liberal Republicans to win. However, the day after Rayburn disclosed his strategy, the Republican Policy Committee announced its opposition and declared its support for Chairman Smith. Vacillating Republicans were called upon to make a difficult choice since committee assignments were yet to be made.[49]

[46] MacNeil, *The Forge of Democracy*, pp. 416–17. *Congressional Quarterly Weekly Report*, January 6, 1961, p. 4.
[47] MacNeil, *The Forge of Democracy*, pp. 419–26.
[48] *Congressional Quarterly Weekly Report*, January 31, 1961, p. 31.
[49] MacNeil, *The Forge of Democracy*, p. 428.

January 25 was selected originally as the day for the showdown vote. As the date approached, it became evident from extensive polling by both sides that the issue would be settled by less than ten votes. In fact, the vote promised to be so close that Speaker Rayburn had it postponed until January 31.

On the day of the crucial vote the gallery was packed to witness one of the most dramatic congressional decisions in years. The debate was limited to one hour and thirty minutes for each side. Smith and his supporters argued against "packing the committee," and the Rayburn forces opposed "frustrating the will of the majority." Finally the long-awaited roll call vote was made, and the House adopted the resolution to enlarge the Rules Committee to fifteen members by a vote of 217 to 212. Rayburn gained all of the 129 Northern and Western Democrats' votes, 66 votes from border and southern states, and 22 Republicans' votes. Smith had gathered 148 Republicans' votes and 64 Democrats' votes, all from southern and border states.[50]

The Speaker was now in a position to "reform" the Rules Committee. He selected Carl Elliott, an Alabama liberal (on economic issues), and B. F. Sisk, a liberal from California, as the two Democratic appointees to the committee. Both men favored federal aid to education, and as Table 24 shows they both voted to expedite school-aid legislation in 1961. Representative Sisk, who remained on the committee, also voted to grant the 1965 bill a rule.

The account of the 1961 school-aid action presented in Chapter III related how this enlargement of the committee failed to prevent the Kennedy aid bills from being killed in the Rules Committee. However, in 1961 it was not the action of a conservative coalition that cut off the bill; it was Representative Delaney, a liberal (but Catholic) committee member, who dealt the fatal blow. Presumably, the federal aid bill would have been processed through the Rules junction had not the religious conflict flared as it did.

In 1963 the House Rules Committee was expanded permanently to fifteen members.[51] This institutional change meant that in 1965 school-aid bills were likely to be granted rules if, among other things, the religious issue were resolved. It is important to note, however, that it was not only vital for the proponents to gain Delaney's vote; they also needed the support of the Protestant Democrats on the Rules Committee in view of

[50] *Congressional Quarterly Weekly Report*, February 3, 1961, pp. 170–71.

[51] For a comparison of the 1961 and 1963 votes see Peabody, "The Enlarged Rules Committee," in Peabody and Polsby, *New Perspectives on the House of Representatives*, pp. 129–64. Carl Elliot died in 1961 and was replaced by John Young of Texas, but this change did not alter the "liberal-conservative" composition of the committee.

the fact that in 1961 Representatives Carl Elliott, Homer Thornberry (Texas), and James Trimble had indicated that they would have voted to table the NDEA amendment bill if Delaney had not joined the conservative coalition to kill all three education bills. Consequently, the fact that the religious issue was generally resolved among the major interest groups probably prevented the blockage of the 1965 school-aid bill in the Rules Committee once again, for Trimble[52] and the three other Protestant Democrats (Richard Bolling, John Young, and Claude Pepper) voted for the 1965 bill. The fruits of the enlargement fight and of the settling of the religious question, then, were realized by the backers of federal aid to education on March 22, 1965, when the Rules Committee voted 8 to 7 to clear the school-aid bill for floor consideration. Clearly, the enlargement of the Rules Committee made such an action possible once the other controversial issues surrounding federal aid were resolved in the House, as they essentially were in 1965.

The alterations within the congressional system discussed in this chapter clearly facilitated the enactment of the 1965 Education Act. The three major changes contributed to the proponent victories at points in the legislative system prior to floor consideration and to a speedy legislative trek for the proposal. This latter point should not be overlooked. The accent on speed stressed by the administration and congressional proponents of the bill stems from the view that if a highly controversial bill can be processed smoothly and quickly it is less likely to be diverted by the several issues involved and ultimately defeated. With a long history of controversy surrounding the question of federal aid to education, it is understandable that the backers of the 1965 bill were eager to have it processed quickly to minimize the possibilities of its fatal entanglement with the perennial issues. Their success—the bill was passed by the House in less than three months—must be explained, in part, by the changes that occurred within the legislative system prior to the introduction of the 1965 proposal.

[52] Trimble was the only one of the three still a member of the House.

VI. Summary and Conclusions

After many years of frustrating failure, the proponents of general federal aid for education finally achieved victory. The Elementary and Secondary Education Act was enacted in 1965. This study has been primarily concerned with identifying the factors that contributed to the passage of this legislation.

In an attempt to organize the many relevant factors into a meaningful pattern, the decision was made to utilize a version of one of the more recent methodological approaches in political science: an input-output systems model. The national legislature was designated as the unit of analysis. The primary task was to indicate which factors impinging upon the legislature and within the legislative system had undergone sufficient change prior to and during 1965 to produce the new output—the Education Act of 1965.

The most fundamental finding that emerges from this endeavor is that the final passage of the school-aid bill cannot be explained by a single major change at the exclusion of others. The long-awaited proponent victory must be viewed in the context of several inextricably interrelated factors. The interdependence among the changes is such that it is not possible to rank them systematically in order of importance in any meaningful fashion. Indeed, it would be a mistake to attempt such a ranking since it would imply a simplified conception of the complex interaction among the factors that made the passage of the proposal possible. All are necessary to explain the outcome; no single variable is sufficient.

Although no ranking of factors is possible, it is instructive to review the major changes and to note their respective contributions to the outcome. It is conceivable that a faltering at any one of the links would have doomed the bill or caused considerable modification of it.

Concerning the changes among the input factors, the Democratic victory in the 1964 election is one of the crucial components of the pattern. As has been demonstrated, the question of federal aid became an increasingly partisan issue, and the ideological gap between the parties was unusually wide during the 1964 campaign. Consequently, the overwhelming Democratic victory provided a solid foundation for the 1965 federal aid effort. The election resulted in a predominantly liberal Congress with a Democratic majority of 36 in the Senate and, most importantly, 155 in the House of Representatives. This congressional line-up meant that the Democrats were presented with an exceptional opportuntiy to deliver on their long-time pledge to enact a federal aid to education program.

Fortunately for the supporters of federal aid, the 1964 election also resulted in another favorable input factor, the re-election of President Lyndon Johnson. This is another key aspect of the pattern since it is apparent that President Johnson was one of the strongest advocates of federal aid and the most astute and persuasive politician to occupy the presidency in the post-World War II period. There is little doubt that he made school aid a top prority item on his legislative agenda for the first session of the Eighty-ninth Congress and provided the necessary leadership to assure enactment of the bill.

Not only was the Johnson administration strongly committed to federal aid, but the President and his associates displayed considerable ingenuity in constructing the bill, working with key interest groups, and devising the strategy for guiding the proposal through the legislative process. Their task in all three respects was simplified by the passage of the Civil Rights Act of 1964, an earlier output of the legislative system which eventually had a "feedback" effect on the 1965 school-aid action. Title VI of the Civil Rights Act outlawed the allocation of federal funds to segregated programs. Consequently, óne controversial component of the federal aid issue was removed as a complicating factor in the building of a consensus for the school-aid bill. Proponents of school aid were free to plan their strategy on the assumption that the proposal would not become seriously entangled with a civil rights amendment as had been the case in 1956 and 1960.

Given the impressive congressional majority and the neutralization of the segregation question, the administration forces assumed the responsibility of drafting an "acceptable" bill—a bill that would gain the support of the major organized interest groups. They concentrated on devising an appropriate formula for resolving another complicating variable: the question of aid to nonpublic schools. The ingredients of such a formula were plain. It was necessary to include some form of assistance that would gain the support of the Catholic organizations yet not alienate the Protestant groups and the National Education Association. The administration wisely decided to include representatives from both sides in working out the approach. Separate and joint conferences were held by the administration officials in the fall of 1964 with the

National Catholic Welfare Conference and the National Education Association. That these meetings were successful was attested to by the simultaneous approval of the bill by these two key organizations on the day President Johnson delivered his education message. Eventually, these organizations were joined in their support of the legislation by most of the major Protestant organizations. The willingness of these groups to compromise on the religious issue was no doubt related to their desire to avert a repetition of the 1961 conflict, to the "ecumenical environment" that had developed, and possibly to the growing support of public opinion on the question of aid to private schools.

Not only did the administration fashion a bill that satisfied both the Catholics and non-Catholics, it also presented a proposal "in tune" with developing circumstances during the mid-1960's. Three major environmental changes occurring in the American society had important consequences for the education function. These changes included the "rediscovery" of poverty in America, the increasing metropolitanization, and the renewed vitality of the civil rights movement. The combination of these changes produced a new political environment and set of inputs to the national legislative system. The drafters of the administration's bill took advantage of these developments and successfully linked the question of federal aid to the problem of poverty in America, to the crisis confronting urban and rural schools, and implicitly to the civil rights revolution. By so doing, they put the issue of federal assistance in a refreshing context which had good chances for gaining widespread support. It is difficult to imagine a proposal that would have had more "political appeal" than the bill presented by the administration. The proposal reflected sensitivity to the major environmental changes which were, and still are, occurring in American society to such an extent that even the opponents of federal aid to education found it difficult to develop a case against the basic concept underpinning the legislation.

The combination of a proposal that simultaneously articulated a response to pressing circumstantial factors and resolved (if only temporarily) the church-state dilemma resulted in an interest group alignment that weighed heavily in favor of the bill's proponents. Whereas the great majority of school-aid supporters backed the bill, the long-time foes of federal aid mustered virtually no resistance to the legislation. In fact, it appears that the staunchest historical opponents of federal aid to education abdicated their position during the 1965 action and viewed resistance as a "lost cause." Consequently, the new group coalition that emerged in 1965 constituted another integral part of the input factors which acted on the national legislature to produce a new response to the educational problems of the nation.

All of these input factors operated in favor of the enactment of the proposed school-aid bill. Their combined pressure made it unlikely that the legislative system would not produce the new policy output. However, changes within the legislative system constituted additional factors which eventually assured that the legislation would not be delayed unduly or endangered by the countless hazards that may erupt while a bill is under consideration. Adam Clayton Powell's appointment as chairman of the House Committee on Education and Labor in place of Graham Barden meant that the administration had a supporter of federal aid at a vital point in the system and could count on cooperation, which it received with a slight delay. The new two-to-one ratio of Democrats and Republicans on the committee, instituted in 1959 and retained in 1965, provided further assurance that favorable committee treatment would be given to the bill. Finally, the enlargement of the House Rules Committee and the resolution of the religious issue among the various groups contributed to favorable committee action and consequently removed the last institutional pitfall in the system which had blocked earlier aid bills.

Considering the mixture of both input and system changes that occurred prior to and during 1965, it would be somewhat surprising if the Elementary and Secondary Education Act had not passed. The trio of system changes which had occurred over a period of three years (1959–61) removed key institutional obstacles and inched the proponents of aid closer and closer to their goal. Once the Rules Committee was enlarged in 1961, the institutional structure per se of the legislative system was no longer a hindrance to the proponents of aid (if, indeed, it ever had been). The next requirement was a cohesive majority that could process a school-aid bill through the relatively streamlined system. The Democratic victory at the congressional level provided the basis for such a majority, and the victory at the presidential level supplied a President who was not only capable of leading the majority but who had the political skill to devise a proposal acceptable to the relevant nongovernmental groups. In sum, all of the major factors were altered in the direction favoring the enactment of school-aid legislation. No single apparent change operated to reduce the chances of the proponents' victory; the ideal pattern finally had meshed.

At a more general level of analysis this account of the passage of the 1965 Education Act provides a source for hypothesizing how major political innovation occurs in relation to the national legislative system. The study suggests that major innovation is likely to result from a series of incremental changes which culminate at a point in time rather than from a single major event. This appears to be the usual case for at least two reasons. First, the legislative system involves a more difficult terrain for proponents of change because they are required to win approval at a series of junctions while opponents need to halt innovation at only a single point. Second, any major controversial issue usually is not a single issue at all, but a group of interrelated controversial issues which must be resolved somehow before the basic change can occur. For example, consensus on federal aid to education as a policy position was not enough; consensus also had to be built on the questions of aid to segregated schools, aid to nonpublic schools, the allocation of aid among the states, and the "appropriate" role of the federal government in the education function. To the extent that other issues also are characterized by a variety of controversial sub-issues, major innovation will generally take place only when it is possible to resolve the component parts. This is likely to involve several incremental changes over a period of time. As each incremental alteration occurs or is accomplished, the proponents of innovation may concentrate their efforts on the remaining hurdles. If they are fortunate and skillful they can be successful.

This study also indicates the significance of the feedback effect of earlier system outputs on pending legislation. The supporters of school aid viewed, with good reason, the 1961 outcome as a major defeat which probably doomed the possibilities of victory in the near future. However, as it turned out, the 1961 action and output did not terminate the efforts to bring about change but actually stimulated the relevant groups to search with a new vitality for a compromise solution. Thus, what appeared to be a negative output eventually had a positive impact on future proceedings.

Similarly, the enactment of the Civil Rights Act of 1964, although it did not directly include references to federal aid to education, had an important feedback effect on the passage of the 1965 school-aid bill. By dealing with the question of federal aid and segregation at the broadest level, it, in effect, removed from consideration (at least for Northern Democrats and Republicans) one of the major issues that had blocked the enactment of earlier bills. In sum, the student of political innovation should be cognizant of the latent implications of earlier outputs for the change he is analyzing.

Finally, this study and some subsequent developments suggest a more speculative, but worth mentioning, hypothesis concerning the kind of political change that has been discussed. It seems that once the proponents achieve victory in an area where they were unsuccessful for a considerable time, they move to expand the magnitude of their victory rapidly. More specifically, the backers of school aid were able to increase considerably the federal government's fiscal commitment to the 1965 program during the 1966 congressional session. In October, 1966, both the House and the Senate passed amended administration bills authorizing new funds under the Education Act of 1965. Although the original administration bill requested an authorization of $1.3 billion for the fiscal year 1967, the House authorized about $1.8 billion and the Senate $2.2 billion for 1967; and the House and Senate authorized $3.5 billion and $3.6 billion, respectively, for 1968. In other words, assuming favorable action by the appropriations committees, federal support for elementary and secondary education would experience a sixfold increase during the first three years of the 1965 law. This action provides strong evidence for considering the Education Act of 1965 as the dreaded breakthrough that opponents of federal aid fought so long. A substantial expansion of the federal government's role in education is now established, and there is reason to believe that it will increase rapidly.

Appendix:

A SUMMARY OF THE ELEMENTARY AND SECONDARY EDUCATION ACT OF 1965

TITLE I: Financial Assistance to Local Educational Agencies for the Education of Children of Low-Income Families

Policy: To provide financial assistance to local educational agencies serving areas with concentrations of children from low-income families to expand and improve their educational programs by various means (including preschool programs) which contribute particularly to meeting the special educational needs of educationally deprived children.

Estimated Funds: $1,174,887,454

Duration: July 1, 1965, to June 30, 1968

Formula: The allocation to each county is computed by adding (a) the number of children aged 5 to 17 from families with incomes of less than $2,000 to (b) the number of children aged 5 to 17 from families receiving an annual income in excess of $2,000 from payments through the program of aid to families with dependent children under Title IV of the Social Security Act and (c) multiplying the sum by one-half the state average per pupil current expenditure during the school year 1963–1964.

Administration: Local educational agencies may receive funds for any fiscal year only upon application therefor approved by the appropriate state educational agency, upon its determination:

(1) that payments will be used for programs and projects of sufficient size, scope, and quality to give reasonable promise of substantial progress toward meeting the special educational needs of children from low-income families;

(2) that the local agency has made provision for including special educational services and arrangements (such as dual enrollment, educational radio and television, and mobile educational services and equipment) in which low-income children attending non-public school can participate;

(3) that a public agency will administer the funds and property acquired under the title;

(4) that the construction of school facilities under the title be consistent with overall state plans for the construction of school facilities;

(5) that effective procedures will be adopted for evaluating at least annually the effectiveness of the programs in meeting the special needs of educationally deprived children;

(6) that the local educational agency will make an annual report to the State educational agency including the above information;

(7) that wherever there is, in the area served by the local educational program, an Anti-Poverty Program, the programs and projects have been developed in cooperation with the public or private non-profit agency responsible for the community action program; and

(8) that effective procedures will be adopted for acquiring and disseminating to teachers and administrators significant information derived from educational research, demonstration, and similar projects, and for adopting, where appropriate, promising educational practices developed through such projects.

TITLE II: School Library Resources, Textbooks, and Other Instructional Material

Policy: To establish a program for making grants for the acquisition of school library resources, textbooks, and other printed and published instructional materials for the use of children and teachers in public and private elementary and secondary schools.

Estimated Funds: $100,000,000 for the fiscal year ending June 30, 1966; the Congress to determine the authorization thereafter.

Distribution: Each state will receive a proportion of the total grant that is equal to that state's proportion of all public and non-public school children enrolled in elementary and secondary schools.

Administration: In order to participate, a State would submit to the Office of Education a plan spelling out criteria to be used in allocating funds within the State. The plan must take into consideration the need of children and teachers for such material and provide assurance that such materials would be provided on an equitable basis for all elementary and secondary school children and teachers. Title to library resources, textbooks, and other printed and published instructional materials furnished pursuant to this title, and control and administration of their use, shall vest only in a public agency.

TITLE III: Supplementary Educational Centers and Services

Policy: To establish a program for making grants to supplementary educational centers and services, to stimulate and assist in the provision of vitally needed educational services not available in sufficient quantity or quality, and to stimulate and assist in the development and establishment of exemplary elementary and secondary school educational programs to serve as models for regular school programs.

Estimated Funds: $75,000,000 for the fiscal year ending June 30, 1966; the Congress to determine the authorization thereafter.

Distribution: Each state would receive a flat grant of $200,000. In addition, each state would receive two more grants based on their proportion of children 5 to 17 and their proportion of the total national population.

Administration: Under this program the local educational agency or agencies apply for a grant through the State Department of Education. The plan, in the establishment and carrying out of the program, must include the participation of persons broadly representative of the cultural and educational resources of the area to be served. The plan may include such educational services as guidance and counseling, remedial instruction, school health services, dual enrollment programs, and specialized instruction in subjects not taught in the local schools. Cultural services may include symphony orchestras, museums, planetariums, theaters, and the like.

TITLE IV: Educational Research and Training

Policy and Funds: The title amends the Cooperative Research Act to authorize $100,000,000 over the next five years for the construction of national and regional research facilities. In addition to the construction funds, there is provision for expansion of the current research programs administered by the Office of Education.

Administration: Grants would be distributed for construction and programs of national and regional research laboratories. Proposals for such grants would be developed by groups representing State departments of education, local school systems, and universities. Programs would basically be located in areas of population concentration where an adequate operating staff may be assembled, but laboratory activities would extend throughout each region.

TITLE V: Grants to Strengthen State Departments of Education

Policy: To establish a program for making grants to stimulate and assist States in strengthening the leadership resources of their State educational agencies, and to assist those agencies in the establishment and improvement of programs to identify and meet the educational needs of the state.

Estimated Funds: $14,450,000 for the fiscal year ending June 30, 1966; the Congress to determine the authorization thereafter.

Distribution: Each State shall receive a $100,000 flat grant and a proportion of 85 per cent of the remaining funds that is equal to its proportion of all public school pupils.

Administration: State departments, when applying for grants, would review their present programs and indicate their greatest needs. Grants could be utilized to improve educational planning; identify special educational problems and needs; evaluate educational programs and any number of projects that would improve the operation of State departments of education and the services they provide to local educational agencies.

Index

AFL-CIO: 33, 54

Aid for instructional material: 5, 67–86, 79–80

Aid formula: 4, 41, 94–96

American Civil Liberties Union: 78–79, 81

American Farm Bureau: 52, 53, 54

American Federation of Teachers: 54, 70n

American Institute for Public Opinion: 43, 46, 47, 49, 50

American Jewish Congress: 54, 55, 78, 80

American Legion: 52, 53, 54, 81

Archer, Glenn L.: 70

Atter, Karl J.: 60

Bailey, Cleveland: 119

Baptist Joint Committee on Public Affairs: 54, 55, 73–74

Barden, Graham A.: 101, 111, 116, 117–20, 134

Bell, Alphonzo: 80, 117

Bendiner, Robert: 2–3, 111n

Bentley, Arthur: 50

Black, Hugo: 58

Bolling, Richard: 130

Brademas, John: 77–78

Brown v. Board of Education: 28, 79, 92

Calendar Wednesday: 66n, 84n, 125

Carlson, C. Emanuel: 73–74

Celebrezze, Anthony J.: 36, 81

Chamber of Commerce: 53, 81, 83, 84

Child-benefit theory: 71, 72n, 81

Cities: *de facto* segregation, 30–31; population growth, 20–21; school problems, 20–28, 37–38; socioeconomic characteristics of inhabitants, 22–26

Citizens for Educational Freedom: 53, 55, 57

Civil Rights Act of 1964: 31–33, 48, 84, 92, 132, 135

Civil rights movement: 10, 11, 28–33, 133

Clark, Joseph S.: 63

Colmer, William: 65, 66, 124, 128

Committee of the Whole (House): 64

Committee on Education and Labor (House): action (1961), 64–65; hearings (1965), 71–80; action (1965), 80; jurisdiction, 113; membership, 113–16; larger federal role, 114–15; decision-making style, 115–16; party ratio, 116–17, 134; chairmen, 117–22

Committee on Labor and Public Welfare (Senate): hearings (1961), 61–63; larger federal role, 114–15

Committee on Rules (House): 64, 65, 66, 84, 94, 105, 110, 111; and federal aid, 122, 124–27; expansion (1961), 127–30

Conant, James B.: 27

Congressional Quarterly: 89–90, 108, 115

Congress of Racial Equality: 29

Connor, Eugene "Bull": 29

Consensus: 1, 2, 61, 114n

Council of Chief State School Officers: 54, 77–78, 80, 81

Council of State Chambers of Commerce: 54

Datt, John: 53

Daughters of the American Revolution: 52, 54, 81

Dawson, William: 33

Delaney, James: 65, 66, 71, 84, 94, 129–30